# THE ENNEAGRAM PERSONALITY PORTRAITS

## Enhancing Professional Relationships

Patrick J. Aspell, Ph.D.
Dee Dee Aspell, M.A.

The opening quotes opposite chapters 1, 3, 4, 5, 6, 10, 14, and 15, appendices A and B, and the "About the Authors" page were reproduced from *The Quotable Woman: An Encyclopedia of Useful Quotations Indexed by Subject and Author* by Elaine Partnow. Published by Corwin Books, Thousand Oaks, CA, 1977.

The opening quotes opposite chapters 2, 7, 8, 9, 11, 12, 13, and 16 were reproduced from *Bartlett's Familiar Quotations: A Collection of Passages, Phrases, and Proverbs Traced to Their Sources in Ancient and Modern Literature* (16th ed.) by John Bartlett. Edited by Justin Kaplan. Published by Little, Brown and Company, New York, NY, 1992.

Printed in the United States of America

### Library of Congress Cataloging-in-Publication Data

Aspell, Patrick J.
    The enneagram personality portraits : enhancing professional relationships / Patrick J. Aspell, Dee Dee Aspell.
        p.    cm.
    Includes bibliographical references and index.
    ISBN: 0-7879-0883-5 (cloth)
    1. Enneagram.   2. Typology (Psychology)   3. Personality and occupation.   I. Aspell, Dee Dee, 1954-    . II. Title.
    BF698.35.E54A87 1997
    155.2'6–dc21                                                                                   96-45887

Published by

350 Sansome Street, 5th Floor
San Francisco, California 94104–1342
(415) 433–1740; Fax (415) 433–0499
(800) 274–4434; Fax (800) 569–0443

Visit our website at: http://www.pfeiffer.com

Outside of the United States, Pfeiffer products can be purchased from the following Simon & Schuster International Offices:

Prentice Hall
Campus 400
Maylands Avenue
Hemel Hempstead
Hertfordshire HP2 7EZ
**United Kingdom**
44(0) 1442 881891; Fax 44(0) 1442 882074

Prentice Hall Professional
Locked Bag 507
Frenchs Forest PO NSW 2086
**Australia**
61 2 9454 2200; Fax 61 2 9453 0089

Simon & Schuster (Asia) Pte Ltd
317 Alexandra Road
#04–01 IKEA Building
Singapore 159965
**Asia**
65 476 4688; Fax 65 378 0370

Prentice Hall/Pfeiffer
P.O. Box 1636
Randburg 2125
**South Africa**
27 11 781 0780; Fax 27 11 781 0781

Printing   10  9  8  7  6  5

# ACKNOWLEDGMENTS

It is said that if we see farther than our ancestors, it is because we stand on the shoulders of those who preceded us. We too are indebted to the teachers and writers who have mined and discovered the hidden riches of the Enneagram: Gurdjieff, Ichazo, Naranjo, Beesing, Condon, Dobson and Hurley, Palmer, Riso, Rohr, and Wagner. All have made original contributions to the development of the Enneagram.

Although we have milked many cows, the butter is our own. We have applied the Enneagram in many unique ways to business and organizations, as well as to education, psychology, and religion. Fortunately, we have been supported on our Enneagram journey by many friends. Our many thanks go out to the following:

- Marian Prokop, who was the prime mover of this Enneagram project and is the expert editor of our works;

- Maryann Morabito, who was an invaluable computer supporter;

- Jack Labanauskas and Andrea Isaacs, co-editors of the *Enneagram Monthly*, who published our many articles on the applications of the Enneagram to business, education, and counseling;

- Maurice and Tolina Doublet, Dee Dee's parents, who have encouraged us through the long years of Enneagram writing;

- David and Juanita Hammeren, our first printers, who believed in us and trusted in our dream;

- All the subjects who graciously consented to take The Enneagram Inventory® from its first version through its many drafts;

- Patrick, our son, whose patience and understanding allows us to devote long hours of labor to give birth to these materials; and

- God, who shared infinite gifts with us and brought our work to fruition.

# CONTENTS

**CHAPTER 1:**
**ORIGINS OF THE ENNEAGRAM**      1

What Is the Enneagram?      1

The Meaning of the Enneagram      2

Benefits of the Enneagram      4

Purpose      4

**CHAPTER 2:**
**ARROWS AND WINGS OF DEVELOPMENT**      7

Beyond Nine Types      7

Arrows of Development      9

Wings of Development      12

Choosing Growth      15

**CHAPTER 3: ENNEAGRAM TYPE ONE**      17

Personality: Perfecter      17

Work Style: Quality Performer      17

Leadership: Stabilizer      18

Thinking Style: Idealist      18

Beliefs and Principles      19

Motivation and Appreciation      19

Professional Development      20

Professional Decline      20

Personal and Professional Empowerment      21

**CHAPTER 4:**
**ENNEAGRAM TYPE TWO**      23

Personality: Carer      23

Work Style: Helper      23

Leadership: Supporter      24

Thinking Style: Affective      24

Beliefs and Principles      24

Motivation and Appreciation 25
Professional Development 25
Professional Decline 26
Personal and Professional Empowerment 27

## CHAPTER 5:
### ENNEAGRAM TYPE THREE 29
Personality: Achiever 29
Work Style: Producer 29
Leadership: Motivator 30
Thinking Style: Practical 30
Beliefs and Principles 30
Motivation and Appreciation 31
Professional Development 31
Professional Decline 32
Personal and Professional Empowerment 33

## CHAPTER 6:
### ENNEAGRAM TYPE FOUR 35
Personality: Creator 35
Work Style: Expressionist 35
Leadership: Personalist 36
Thinking Style: Individualist 36
Beliefs and Principles 37
Motivation and Appreciation 37
Professional Development 37
Professional Decline 38
Personal and Professional Empowerment 39

## CHAPTER 7:
### ENNEAGRAM TYPE FIVE 41
Personality: Observer 41
Work Style: Thinker 41

Leadership: Systematizer 42

Thinking Style: Analytical 42

Beliefs and Principles 42

Motivation and Appreciation 43

Professional Development 43

Professional Decline 44

Personal and Professional Empowerment 45

**CHAPTER 8:**
    **ENNEAGRAM TYPE SIX** 47

Personality: Groupist 47

Work Style: Relater 47

Leadership: Teamster 48

Thinking Style: Group Minded 48

Beliefs and Principles 49

Motivation and Appreciation 49

Professional Development 49

Professional Decline 50

Personal and Professional Empowerment 51

**CHAPTER 9:**
    **ENNEAGRAM TYPE SEVEN** 53

Personality: Cheerer 53

Work Style: Animator 53

Leadership: Cheerleader 54

Thinking Style: Positive 54

Beliefs and Principles 55

Motivation and Appreciation 55

Professional Development 56

Professional Decline 56

Personal and Professional Empowerment 57

## CHAPTER 10:
### ENNEAGRAM TYPE EIGHT     59

Personality: Challenger     59

Work Style: Asserter     59

Leadership: Director     60

Thinking Style: Dialectical     60

Beliefs and Principles     61

Motivation and Appreciation     61

Professional Development     62

Professional Decline     62

Personal and Professional Empowerment     63

## CHAPTER 11:
### ENNEAGRAM TYPE NINE     65

Personality: Accepter     65

Work Style: Receptionist     65

Leadership: Reconciler     66

Thinking Style: Holistic     66

Beliefs and Principles     66

Motivation and Appreciation     67

Professional Development     67

Professional Decline     68

Personal and Professional Empowerment     69

## CHAPTER 12:
### TYPES IN RELATIONSHIPS     71

Introduction     71

ONES     72

TWOS     75

THREES     78

FOURS     80

FIVES     83

SIXES     87

SEVENS                                      90

EIGHTS                                      93

NINES                                       96

CHAPTER 13:

    ENNEAGRAM AND COLORS        **101**

    Perfecters and White                101

    Carers and Pink                     101

    Achievers and Green                 102

    Creators and Purple                 102

    Observers and Gray                  103

    Groupists and Brown                 103

    Cheerers and Yellow                 104

    Challengers and Red                 104

    Accepters and Blue                  105

CHAPTER 14:

    APPLICATIONS OF THE ENNEAGRAM   **107**

    Studying Enneagram Types            107

    Training Applications               108

    For More Information                111

CHAPTER 15:

    FUTURE DIRECTIONS               **113**

    Empowerment                         113

    Personal and Professional Style     113

SELECTED BIBLIOGRAPHY                       **119**

APPENDIX A:

    SUMMARY CHARTS OF KEY TRAITS    **123**

APPENDIX B:

    SUMMARY CHARTS OF CONGRUENCE    **133**

ABOUT THE AUTHORS                           **143**

INDEX                                       **145**

*"The greatness of the human personality begins at the hour of birth."*

— Maria Montessori

# 1

# ORIGINS OF THE ENNEAGRAM

## WHAT IS THE ENNEAGRAM?

The cutting edge technology of the Enneagram (pronounced "ANY-a-gram") system describes nine personality types and professional styles of thinking, feeling, acting, and relating. (See Figure 1.) This is a system whose time has come for the business world. Emerging as a

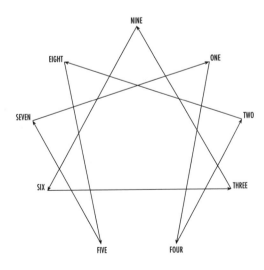

**Figure 1. The Enneagram**

powerful tool for empowering organizations, executives, managers, consultants, and trainers; it is increasingly being used by businesses throughout the world for managing, motivating, and training people.

Professional style flows from personality. Who a person is determines how he or she will act. Actions are expressions of being, and basic character explains behavior. Recall that ancient philosophical imperative of Socrates: "Know thyself." If you know yourself—your thoughts, feelings, desires, motivations—you will know how you are going to behave. For example, if a person is by nature assertive, he or she will tend to behave in a decisive, forceful manner. Likewise, the substance of an individual's personality underlies his or her style of leadership or work.

## THE MEANING OF THE ENNEAGRAM

The word comes from two Greek words: ennea, meaning "nine," and grammos, meaning "letters" or "points." The Enneagram posits nine personality types, nine ways of experiencing the world. It describes how they function and how they interact with one another.

### Foundations of the Enneagram

The roots of the Enneagram go back many centuries. According to most researchers, the Enneagram originated in the ancient Middle East and developed in Sufism, the mystical tradition of Islam.

George I. Gurdjieff (ca. 1877-1949) and Oscar Ichazo (b. 1931), spiritual teachers, are credited with introducing the Enneagram to the West. Claudio Naranjo, a Chilean psychiatrist, and John Lilly, M.D., brought the system to the United States. Other teachers and researchers, particularly those identified in the acknowledgments of this book, have added their individual interpretations and made unique contributions to our understanding of the Enneagram.

Most recently, the Enneagram has received increased attention from the corporate world. For example, in 1994, Stanford University hosted the First International Enneagram Conference. As one of its key tracks, the conference included a business track that focused on the value and applications of the Enneagram in organizations.

## Enneagram Theory

The Enneagram theory provides a unique model of personalities and professional styles. The psychology of the Enneagram model contrasts your everyday, personal ego and your unique, essential self.

Your personal ego is expressed in distinct and changing ways, using expressions such as "I see," "I feel," "I imagine," "I choose," and so on. You experience yourself as a subject that changes and differs with each distinct experience at different times in different places.

At the same time, you experience yourself as being an individual unique self to whom all of these particular "I's" and activities belong. This unifying source and subject of the many "I's" is your essential self or being. (See Figure 2.) All of the attributes of the nine types are virtually found in each personality. It is your unique, central self that implicitly embraces all the traits of the nine types. Although you may be well empowered in one professional style, you can draw on the inner riches of other styles. For example, an assertive leader can actualize the profound potentialities of his or her essence and become a caring and supportive leader.

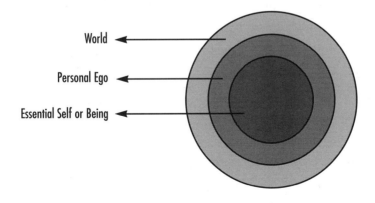

World ←
Personal Ego ←
Essential Self or Being ←

**Figure 2. Core of Personality**

## Benefits of the Enneagram

The ideas of the Enneagram are gaining increasing attention from counselors, trainers, psychologists, and spiritual teachers. The Enneagram offers multiple benefits to professional people—executives and managers, supervisors and employees, educators, and clergy. It provides both an opportunity to appreciate and empower personal professional style.

To professional people and organizations, the Enneagram offers the following insights:

- Provides an objective framework of human behavior.
- Recognizes the value of individual differences.
- Identifies the strengths and the imitations of different professional styles.
- Is understood clearly and easily.
- Builds understanding regarding aspects of an organization.
- Helps to optimize the fit between a person and his or her professional position.
- Has profitable applications for areas such as communication conflict management, motivation, ways of thinking, interpersonal relationships, team building, problem solving, and time management.
- Helps people discover and empower their personalities and professional styles.
- Builds a stable framework for emotional issues.
- Helps people to be more effective in relationships.
- Enables people to improve their motivation levels.

## Purpose

The purpose of this book is to describe the background of the Enneagram, the nine personality types and professional styles, potential applications of the Enneagram, and directions for the future. Different facets of each type and style are brought to light in order to appreciate the riches of each. This book can be used in a variety of situations, including leadership development, work improvement, relationship enhancement, team building, organizational improvement, career empowerment, problem solving, and personal growth.

*"Why stay we on the earth except to grow?"*

— Robert Browning

# 2

# Arrows and Wings of Development

## Beyond Nine Types

Knowledge of the basic Enneagram types is the starting point for understanding yourself and others. However, Enneagram theory offers far more additional rich data for further personal growth and interpersonal development.

One ingredient for deeper awareness of the Enneagram is an understanding of what the psychologist Carl Jung termed "shadow and light." Each Enneagram type has characteristics that lead a person toward a more fulfilling life as well as characteristics that lead a person to a less fulfilling life.

Quite often, the shadow and light characteristics are the same; they differ only in the degree to which they are exhibited in a particular situation. For example, a ONE's desire for accuracy may be an admirable trait in a work situation. However, carried to an extreme, this desire may lead that person to be intolerant of others' failings. Similar analogies can be made for every descriptor applied to every type. A simple way to demonstrate this is to attach the word "overly" or the word "too" to the specific descriptor. For instance, although it may be very flattering to be described as "analytical" or "sensitive" or "spontaneous," the connotation changes when the description is "too analytical" or "overly sensitive" or "too spontaneous."

According to the Enneagram, no individual is an unmixed personality type. Some of the additional information that can be gleaned from careful attention to the Enneagram results from studying the arrows and wings of development, especially from the perspective of shadow and light.

*Arrows* are part of the basic Enneagram diagram: One arrow points toward each type and represents the direction of development; one arrow leads away from each type and represents the direction of decline. *Wings,* in turn, represent the two types adjacent to each of the nine Enneagram types.

Therefore, each Enneagram type has four other types as influences, as follows:

- ONES have FOUR and SEVEN respectively as arrows of decline and development; ONES have NINE and TWO as wings of development.

- TWOS have EIGHT and FOUR respectively as arrows of decline and development; TWOS have ONE and THREE as wings of development.

- THREES have NINE and SIX respectively as arrows of decline and development; THREES have TWO and FOUR as wings of development.

- FOURS have TWO and ONE respectively as arrows of decline and development; FOURS have THREE and FIVE as wings of development.

- FIVES have SEVEN and EIGHT respectively as arrows of decline and development; FIVES have FOUR and SIX as wings of development.

- SIXES have THREE and NINE respectively as arrows of decline and development; SIXES have FIVE and SEVEN as wings of development.

- SEVENS have ONE and FIVE respectively as arrows of decline and development; SEVENS have SIX and EIGHT as wings of development.

- EIGHTS have FIVE and TWO respectively as arrows of decline and development; EIGHTS have SEVEN and NINE as wings of development.

- NINES have SIX and THREE respectively as arrows of decline and development; NINES have EIGHT and ONE as wings of development.

## ARROWS OF DEVELOPMENT

The arrows on the Enneagram diagram refer to the directions of development and decline for each type. Therefore, starting with your dominant type, you can use this information to choose a path to development or a path to decline.

The direction of development involves traveling against the arrow that points toward your style. In the basic Enneagram diagram (see page 1), the direction of development is the path that can be traced from 1 to 7 to 5 to 8 to 2 to 4 to 1, and the path from 9 to 3 to 6 to 9. In terms of shadow and light, this means taking on the beneficial characteristics of that style.

In contrast, the direction of decline involves following the arrow that points away from your basic Enneagram style. This is the direction to which people tend to revert when they are under stress—an unhealthy and frustrating direction. Keep in mind here again the idea of shadow and light. No type is inherently unhealthy or bad. Instead, the direction of decline refers to the tendency to take on the shadow characteristics of a particular style. The following sections outline some specific dimensions that people can take on as they journey toward growth or decline.

## ONES

*Direction of Decline.* Under stress, ONES can revert to the life-draining characteristics of FOURS, tending toward moods, emotions, and envy.

*Direction of Development.* For growth, ONES need to strive toward the life-giving characteristics of SEVENS, embracing new ideas, fun, and optimism.

## TWOS

*Direction of Decline.* Under stress, TWOS can revert to the life-draining characteristics of EIGHTS, tending toward bossiness, arguing, and control.

*Direction of Development.* For growth, TWOS need to strive toward the life-giving characteristics of FOURS, embracing sensitivity, creativity, and compassion.

## THREES

*Direction of Decline.* Under stress, THREES revert to life-draining characteristics of NINES, tending toward laziness, avoidance, and passivity.

*Direction of Development.* For growth, THREES need to strive toward the life-giving characteristics of SIXES, embracing loyalty, commitment, and cooperation.

## FOURS

*Direction of Decline.* Under stress, FOURS can revert to the life-draining characteristics of TWOS, tending toward possessiveness, jealousy, and manipulation.

*Direction of Development.* For growth, FOURS need to strive toward the life-giving characteristics of ONES, embracing objectivity, stability, and self-discipline.

## FIVES

*Direction of Decline.*   Under stress, FIVES can revert to the life-draining characteristics of SEVENS, tending toward fantasy, instability, and indulgence.

*Direction of Development.*   For growth, FIVES need to strive toward the life-giving characteristics of EIGHTS, embracing confidence, leadership, and self-discipline.

## SIXES

*Direction of Decline.*   Under stress, SIXES can revert to the life-draining characteristics of THREES, tending toward impulsiveness, opportunism, and deception.

*Direction of Development.*   For growth, SIXES need to strive toward the life-giving characteristics of NINES, embracing empathy, peace, and acceptance.

## SEVENS

*Direction of Decline.*   Under stress, SEVENS can revert to the life-draining characteristics of ONES, tending toward perfectionism, criticism, and intolerance.

*Direction of Development.*   For growth, SEVENS need to strive toward the life-giving characteristics of FIVES, embracing insight, observation, and understanding.

## EIGHTS

*Direction of Decline.*   Under stress, EIGHTS can revert to the life-draining characteristics of FIVES, tending toward withdrawal, fear, and disconnectedness.

*Direction of Development.* For growth, EIGHTS need to strive toward the life-giving characteristics of TWOS, embracing caring, helpfulness, and sensitivity.

## NINES

*Direction of Decline.* Under stress, NINES can revert to the life-draining characteristics of SIXES, tending toward indecision, suspicions, and overdependence.

*Direction of Development.* For growth, NINES need to strive toward the life-giving characteristics of THREES, embracing motivation, productivity, and energy.

## WINGS OF DEVELOPMENT

In addition to a dominant type, an arrow of decline, and an arrow of development, each individual is characterized by an auxiliary type called the "wing." The wings are those types immediately on either side of the basic dominant type. For instance, a FIVE can have a FOUR-wing or a SIX-wing.

Both wings can affect a particular type. For example, a FIVE can participate in the sensitivity of a FOUR or in the loyalty of a SIX. The assertive EIGHT may share in the calmness of a NINE or in the fun-loving behavior of a SEVEN. Participation in the wings gives each individual his or her distinctive personality subtype.

One of the wings tends to predominate in the personality, while the other functions at least potentially. Thus, for example, a FOUR who is detached like a FIVE has the potentiality of becoming involved like a THREE. As a consequence, in addition to the nine basic types, there are eighteen subtypes (each of the nine basic types can have one of two wings, and 9 x 2 = 18). The following sections outline some specific characteristics of each subtype.

## ONES

*NINE-wing Dominant.*   ONES with a stronger NINE-wing are likely to be more peaceful, relaxed, and easy going.

*TWO-wing Dominant.*   ONES with a stronger TWO-wing are likely to be more caring, compassionate, and concerned for others.

## TWOS

*ONE-wing Dominant.*   TWOS with a stronger ONE-wing are likely to be more task oriented, idealistic, and judgmental.

*THREE-wing Dominant.*   TWOS with a stronger THREE-wing are likely to be more gregarious, competitive, and project focused.

## THREES

*TWO-wing Dominant.*   THREES with a stronger TWO-wing are likely to be more collaborative, friendly, and concerned for others.

*FOUR-wing Dominant.*   THREES with a stronger FOUR-wing are likely to be more creative, responsive, and show more feelings.

## FOURS

*THREE-wing Dominant.*   FOURS with a stronger THREE-wing are likely to be more efficient, active, and enterprising.

*FIVE-wing Dominant.*   FOURS with a stronger FIVE-wing are likely to be more logical, detached, and analytical.

## FIVES

*FOUR-wing Dominant.*   FIVES with a stronger FOUR-wing are likely to be more sensitive, intuitive, and connected with personal feelings.

*SIX-wing Dominant.* FIVES with a stronger SIX-wing are likely to be more dutiful, committed, and identified with a group.

## SIXES

*FIVE-wing Dominant.* SIXES with a stronger FIVE-wing are likely to be more introverted, intellectual, and cautious.

*SEVEN-wing Dominant.* SIXES with a stronger SEVEN-wing are likely to be more playful, spontaneous, and innovative.

## SEVENS

*SIX-wing Dominant.* SEVENS with a stronger SIX-wing are likely to be more moderate, persistent, and attentive to duty.

*EIGHT-wing Dominant.* SEVENS with a stronger EIGHT-wing are likely to be more aggressive, competitive, and controlling.

## EIGHTS

*SEVEN-wing Dominant.* EIGHTS with a stronger SEVEN-wing are likely to be more joyful, responsive, and extroverted.

*NINE-wing Dominant.* EIGHTS with a stronger NINE-wing are likely to be more calm, relaxed, and receptive.

## NINES

*EIGHT-wing Dominant.* NINES with a stronger EIGHT-wing are likely to be more assertive, confrontational, and energetic.

*ONE-wing Dominant.* NINES with a stronger ONE-wing are likely to be more objective, critical, and task oriented.

## Choosing Growth

The development of personal talents can lead to imbalance in some people. Succeeding with a particular personal talent usually makes a person favor that gift and use time, energy, and experiences in developing it. In other words, once we have developed particular strengths and abilities, we are apt to over-rely on them, limiting ourselves. Wanting to travel a familiar road is natural; it takes effort to try something new.

For example, if you are an EIGHT, you tended to learn early in childhood that you obtained rights and fulfilled needs by exercising control and taking charge. Because "nothing succeeds like success," you may have consistently practiced controlling situations and people.

However, your emphasis on a dominant aspect of your personality may have led to neglect of other traits. In your emphasis on control, you may have become too aggressive or fallen instinctively into reacting with anger, especially under stress. If so, you may need to balance control with other traits, such as optimism and relaxation.

In balancing, you call on potential resources that lay dormant in your personality. You develop more options in responding to situations. For example, the balanced EIGHT or Challenger responds with gentleness as well as strength, agreeableness as well as confrontation.

Every person participates in all the talents of all the types. The core of your personality, your essential self, potentially contains the nine Enneagram personalities. In your youth, you developed at least one of those personalities. For example, the Achiever learned that by accomplishing things, needs would be met. A child who gets parental attention and acceptance by scoring good grades in school learns to repeat  behaviors and develops the trait of achievement. As adults, however, each person has the opportunity to actualize the potentialities of any of the personality types.

*"Excellence in life seems to be the way in which each human being makes the most of the adventure of living and becomes most truly and deeply himself."*

— Eda J. LeShan

# 3

# Enneagram Type ONE

## Personality: Perfecter

The personality of ONES can be described as "Perfecters." They strive for excellence in their work. Because they are endowed with a strong moral sense of right and wrong, ONES strive to be correct, just, and truthful. With high ideals and values, they like to improve themselves and others so that the world can be a better place to live. As children, they learned to get approval by conforming to standards.

## Work Style: Quality Performer

ONES are quality performers who want a job to be done well. Conscientious about doing projects correctly, they work hard and stay on task for a long time. They want their work to be done right.

Because they want to finish projects on time, they prefer not to be interrupted by casual conversation in person or on the telephone. They are accurate and precise with details, sometimes to the point of slowing down projects. It is important for ONES to think of themselves as right and good.

ONES like roles and responsibilities to be clearly described according to established guidelines. They tend to be uncomfortable in unstructured situations in which people express controversial opinions and risk being wrong. When they are unsure of the right procedures, they delay making decisions.

Important elements in an organization are order among people and tasks and performing operations according to proper procedures. ONES focus their attention on the correct ordering of tasks, the quality of work, and fairness among people.

## LEADERSHIP: STABILIZER

As people who want to do well in life, ONES naturally tend to be Stabilizers. They stabilize a group or organization by being sure that it conforms to standards of excellence. Their criticisms are intended to ensure that an organization is run correctly, at which point they can fully commit themselves. From start to finish, they want to be certain that each stage in the completion of a project follows the right procedures and measures up to clear criteria. Once convinced that their way is right, they can withstand opposition and persevere until a job is done. Their thinking is logical, as they take one step at a time in coming to conclusions.

Stabilizers usually have clear ideas of how much time a task will take. Methodical and organized, ONES are apt to break complex projects into simple steps. Their thorough attention to detail guarantees that jobs will be done correctly and that products and/or services will be done according to quality standards. When they see ways of living up to their ideals, ONES are likely to work to improve their leadership abilities. It also is important for them to be fair with people.

## THINKING STYLE: IDEALIST

The thinking style of ONES is idealist. Motivated by high standards and values, they think of the extent to which people and organizations measure up to their ideals. Their moral thinking challenges others as well as themselves to live well and work well. They are apt to appeal to principles as the basis of their conclusions. However, anger may prevent them from focusing on facts.

## BELIEFS AND PRINCIPLES

ONES are methodical and alert in managing an organization. Able to think rationally and conscientiously, they make effective organizers. ONES decide what is worthwhile and can hold fast against opposition to their decisions. Concerned with quality control, they make what is good, better and what is better, the best.

Underlying the ONES' work and leadership styles are basic beliefs and principles. They believe that what is worth doing is worth doing well. Another key belief of ONES is that an organization must be run correctly according to rules and regulations in order to function effectively. ONES are concerned about the quality of products and services. They follow the principle that products and services should measure up to high standards.

## MOTIVATION AND APPRECIATION

Motivated by fear of being criticized, ONES strive to be right in their behavior. Intent on living up to high ideals, they want to treat others fairly and better the world. To avoid mistakes, ONES try to control their environments and justify their positions. Wanting to feel free of guilt, they may criticize others for their shortcomings.

ONES value honesty, competence, and industry. Drawn by high standards and principles, they have high regard for integrity and personal responsibility and want to treat people fairly. Their work is usually accurate and neat. ONES appreciate approval when they do what is right. They also have a need to be recognized by competent people for their quality performance. Rapport is created when ONES feel appreciated.

## PROFESSIONAL DEVELOPMENT

ONES develop their professional styles by affirming themselves with positive statements such as "I am fair and right." They also empower their professionalism by journeying toward the SEVEN, adopting positive outlooks toward life and work. This enables them to focus on the good in themselves and in the world.

Another direction of growth for ONES lies in developing their wings. From NINES, ONES learn to be calm when things are not as perfect as they might like; from TWOS, they learn to correct others in caring, helpful ways.

## PROFESSIONAL DECLINE

ONES can become ineffective when they fall into being dogmatic and judgmental. They may revert to anger to motivate others, emphasize rules, and demand progress reports. Because of their fear of making mistakes, ONES may tend not to take risks.

They decline as they become perfectionists, rigid in the ways in which they think, and compulsive in their wanting things to be done properly. When ONES regress toward the FOUR, they become oversensitive, self-doubting, and melancholic. In their work styles, ONES may become self-preoccupied Individualists as well as Perfectionists. In their leadership styles, they may slip into being unrealistic Idealists.

## Personal and Professional Empowerment

For personal and professional empowerment, ONES are invited to consider the following suggestions:

- Set reachable goals with realistic ideas of other people's abilities.

- Take yourself lightly and humorously.

- Be open to the positive potential in a situation as well as what can happen by following operational procedures.

- Claim your anger, acknowledge it as your reaction to imperfection, soften it with sympathy for human limitations, and channel it into constructive criticism.

- Motivate people through appreciation and clear direction rather than harsh criticism.

- Search for the good, and you may be pleasantly surprised to find it.

- Learn to relax in body and mind so you can accomplish your tasks calmly.

- Remember that it's perfectly human to have human imperfection.

- Be willing to adapt and innovate, despite the risk of making mistakes.

- Listen to others' ideas attentively and sensitively.

- Be open to doing things differently.

- Keep in mind that perfection is more a process than a product.

*"There is only one happiness in life, to love and be loved."*

— George Sand

# 4

## ENNEAGRAM TYPE TWO

### PERSONALITY: CARER

TWOS tend to love, care for, and help others. With sincere feeling for others' needs, they are generous in serving, even if it means putting their own interests aside. When they feel loved and cared for, they feel content and worthwhile. Their greatest fear is to be rejected. TWOS grew up learning to cope with family life by helping their caregivers.

### WORK STYLE: HELPER

TWOS are people-oriented individuals who make people feel welcome and comfortable in an organization. Ready to help others at work, people depend on them. They feel at home in a workplace in which they can respond to others' needs. When decisions are being made, TWOS are concerned with how people are going to be affected. They support the decisions of the people in authority in order to ally with them and receive their gratitude.

## Leadership: Supporter

TWOS are Supporters in their leadership styles. Warm and friendly individuals, they mix easily with people in groups and make them feel at home in an organization. Their empathy makes people feel that someone in the organization cares about them personally. They are concerned about problems other people have, whether the problems are work-related or personal difficulties.

TWOS are available to help people when they need advice or encouragement. They keep in mind how their decisions impact on other people. Other workers tend to depend on TWOS for assistance. TWOS are attracted to opportunities in which they can receive approval, especially from important people. They like to be thanked for the help they have given others.

## Thinking Style: Affective

The thinking of TWOS is affective. Motivated to care, they think of what is helpful to others and how they can express warmth and friendliness. For TWOS, the heart has reasons of which the mind knows not. However, their feelings may easily sway their thinking and make them inconsistent in what they say. Their thinking is usually more oriented towards people than things.

## Beliefs and Principles

TWOS have a gift of building rapport with people. They do this with empathy, encouragement, support, praise, and finding the good in others. A basic belief of TWOS is that the strength of an organization lies in its people's feeling cared for and valued. Such people are more apt to have good morale and be productive.

TWOS value caring and being cared for. When they meet people, they want to come across as friendly and warmhearted. They give of themselves, their time, energy, and ideas. They are ready to compliment and praise other people for their good work. Deep inside, TWOS are looking for closeness with other people.

## Motivation and Appreciation

Love and caring motivate TWOS. Love or caring from others makes them feel accepted. They are driven to help others so that they can receive the appreciation they believe they deserve. TWOS want to express their feelings to others in order to feel close to them.

TWOS appreciate being needed and having others depend on them. As a result of helping others in need, TWOS like to receive the personal gratitude and approval that means so much to them.

## Professional Development

TWOS develop their professional styles as well as their personalities by becoming more unselfish and generous in giving of themselves for the good of others. They need to travel toward the characteristics of the life-giving FOUR and become aware of their own genuine feelings and real needs. In their working style, they learn to be Expressionists (like the FOURS) as well as Helpers. When TWOS who are leaders move towards the FOUR, they may become Personalists as well as Supporters. They thereby acknowledge their aggressions and their need to be needed by others.

Because they are aware of their own goodness, TWOS love themselves and relate to others in honest, mutual, and satisfying ways. Healthy TWOS affirm themselves with positive self-talk, such as "I am caring and helpful."

TWOS can also empower their leadership style by cultivating their "wings," the styles of the ONE and THREE. Development of either wing enables TWOS to become task oriented and learn to balance the demands of the job with the needs of people.

## Professional Decline

Under stress, TWOS may manipulate others by flattery. Unaware of their personal needs, TWOS may deny that they have any ulterior motives other than helping others. Caught up with their own self-giving, they tend to overrate what they do for others and think they do more for others than others do for them. Some TWOS want to be informed about everything so they will not miss an opportunity to support others and have them feel obligated.

The style of TWOS declines when they become overly solicitous and intrude into the lives of other people. They tend to flood others with attention and flattery. They appear to be self-sacrificing, creating needs to fulfill and exhausting themselves for others; yet in reality they are jealously trying to possess those they care for.

Under stress, TWOS are apt to move towards the life-draining EIGHT and become domineering and angry. Losing touch with their gentleness, they become hardened and lash out at people who have not responded to their needs. People close to angry TWOS are apt to feel their wrath. In their working styles, they can tend to be Bullies. In this way, TWOS who are leaders can become Dictators like the life-draining EIGHT.

## Personal and Professional Empowerment

For personal and professional empowerment, TWOS are invited to consider the following suggestions:

- Balance your talent for relationships with task skills and technical data.

- Respect other people as valuable in themselves.

- Learn to make objective appraisals and reasonable decisions that are not biased by human factors.

- Let your caring be as unselfish as possible, for it is in genuinely giving that you will receive.

- Accept task-oriented people who may not be as friendly and personable as you are.

- Balance others' needs with your own genuine needs.

- Strengthen your emotional boundaries so you do not over-identify with others' feelings or responsibilities.

- Help people fulfill their genuine needs rather than what you believe will satisfy them.

- Be receptive to feedback that may not be given as gently as you might like.

- Let your true self—your goodness, love, and generosity— draw others to you.

- Use your head rather than your feelings to focus on the organization's priorities.

- Prioritize your caring, beginning with those closest to you and extending to those further from you.

"*Our deeds still travel with us from afar, and what we have been makes us what we are.*"

— George Eliot

# 5

## ENNEAGRAM TYPE THREE

### PERSONALITY: ACHIEVER

THREES are driven to achieve. They aim to succeed by setting forth goals and efficiently organizing their efforts to reach their objectives. High on energy, Achievers are competitive and usually effective in communicating with others. As children, they learned to get attention for their accomplishments.

### WORK STYLE: PRODUCER

THREES want results, and they enjoy talking with others about how to get jobs done. Energetic, they compete with others and work efficiently to complete projects. They may get so caught up in finishing task after task that they become "workaholics."

They usually want to obtain results as quickly as possible, even if it means working under pressure. As a consequence, they may cut corners and lower the quality of their work. It is important for them to make a favorable impression on others in order to be liked. They hope to advance their careers by being productive and admired.

## LEADERSHIP: MOTIVATOR

THREES are usually able to motivate themselves and others in order to succeed. They are persuasive enough to serve as catalysts to motivate others to accomplish tasks. They decide rather quickly about how to use the resources available for a project. THREES are willing to stand up to opposition by people in authority in order to push their projects.

In addition, THREES are usually good socializers who mix well with people and recall their names and faces. Good at meeting and greeting people, they usually make a winning impression. Consequently, they like talking with workers about goals and progress in order to stir interest and enthusiasm. Driven by the desire for success and recognition, THREES relentlessly pursue their objectives until they reach them.

## THINKING STYLE: PRACTICAL

THREES are practical in their thinking. Motivated to achieve, they think of the results they want to produce and calculate the means necessary. Their ideas are tools to put their plans into action. However, THREES may be tempted to compromise integrity to make an idea work for their benefit.

## BELIEFS AND PRINCIPLES

THREES have abilities to accomplish tasks and to relate to people. With clear goals, they are able to calculate what is useful for what they want. Animated by a belief in themselves, THREES market themselves and then their product or services. Because they mix so well with people and present themselves in such a favorable way, they make good communicators.

For THREES, competition brings the best people to the top of an organization, so they motivate themselves and others. They are governed by the principle that winners are highly motivated to get results.

A corollary of that principle is that their enthusiasm and drive motivates others who, in turn, tend to be very productive.

THREES value the things that accompany success and status: sense of accomplishment, fulfillment of ambition, and feeling of self-satisfaction. Through self-improvement, they intend to rise above others and be admired.

## Motivation and Appreciation

Deep inside, THREES are usually driven by the desire to be liked by others. Consequently, they devote a great deal of energy to creating an attractive image of themselves. In that way they can be assured of acceptance by others. Unfortunately, their tendency to use people may bring about the very thing they fear most—rejection. For THREES, the way to authentic growth starts with accepting themselves.

Underlying this drive for success and enterprise, THREES are striving to satisfy needs for recognition, affirmation, and acceptance. The recognition that comes with prestige and status boosts their feelings of superiority and their self-esteem.

## Professional Development

THREES develop their personalities and work styles by positive self-affirmations, such as "I am an Achiever and Producer," and "I am a worthwhile and likable person." They can empower their working styles by journeying toward the life-giving SIX, seeing themselves as part of a larger whole within which they are aware of group interests. By being committed to others and cooperative, they receive affirmation from others and deepen their sense of self-worth. As they give and receive, THREES learn the value of relationships for themselves and others. In their work styles, THREES become Relaters as well as Producers; in leadership, they become Teamsters as well as Motivators.

Another road to enrichment lies in developing their wings, that is, the TWO and FOUR. From the life-giving TWO-wing, THREES can learn to be helpful to others as well as concerned about their individual interests. When THREES develop their life-giving FOUR-wing, they come to realize that they themselves are special people.

## PROFESSIONAL DECLINE

THREES can fall into the trap of being more style than substance, appearing better than they actually are. Afraid of failure, they are apt to exploit others in order to reach or stay on top. They can become hostile towards competitors or those who threaten their advancement. When their desires to succeed get out of hand, they may become Opportunists who take advantage of situations for their own benefit. Because THREES are apt to persist in their endeavors in order to succeed, they can easily become "workaholics."

With tendencies to be out of contact with their feelings and obsessed with status and prestige, THREES may sacrifice close relationships for success in their work. If they journey in the direction of decline, they tend to become self-centered and Opportunists. When they fall into the ways of the life-draining NINE, they are apt to numb their angry feelings so as to appease others to gain acceptance. In their work styles, THREES who slip towards the life-draining NINE may become Passivists as well as Opportunists; in their leadership styles then, they become Appeasers.

# PERSONAL AND PROFESSIONAL EMPOWERMENT

For personal and professional empowerment, THREES are invited to consider the following suggestions:

- Accept yourself as you are with your talents and abilities.

- Respect other people as valuable in themselves, not to be used simply as means to an end.

- Look beyond self-interests to the common good of the team, group, organization, or family by animating, organizing, recognizing, and promoting talents of individual members.

- Moderate your energies in order to maintain your health and consistent productivity.

- Be clear about the meaning of success so that short-term outcomes are in step with long-range goals.

- Respect others' ways of thinking, planning, and acting.

- Base your goals on clear values and priorities so you can be sure of how you want to live and work.

- Perceive people more as collaborative than as competitive, for friends work better together than opponents.

- Accurately state what you have truly achieved, for as Shakespeare wrote, "To thine own self be true, and as sure as night follows day, thou canst not help but be true to others."

- Balance task skills with interpersonal concerns.

- Acknowledge, affirm, and motivate others, and you will receive affirmation and support, for it is in giving that you receive.

- Remember that quality complements quantity.

*"The artist has always been and still is a being somewhat apart from the rest of humanity."*

— Beatrice Hinkle

# 6

# ENNEAGRAM TYPE FOUR

## PERSONALITY: CREATOR

FOURS are naturally introspective and aware of their feelings and impulses. They take time with themselves to deepen their self-awareness. When they are in contact with the light and dark sides of their nature, they can be genuine, unique, and creative in their expressions of feelings. Their sensitivity finds expression in their consideration of others. As children, they learned to feel unique because of the special attention they received.

## WORK STYLE: EXPRESSIONIST

Usually aware of their own feelings, FOURS tend to be expressive in communicating with people. They like to be open about how they feel about projects, and their interest in a task may alternate between highs and lows.

The work environment of a FOUR may have quite a distinctive appearance. Because they are imaginative in their approaches to tasks, they may create unique results. When they are singled out for their special talents and recognized by distinguished persons, they are very motivated in their work. FOURS dislike doing the ordinary work that offers no opportunity for recognition, especially from important people. In addition, their work pace may slow when they are in low moods. FOURS prefer to acquire special skills for dealing with unique situations, and they respect people who hold prominent positions of authority.

FOURS focus on individuals in an organization. They are very much aware of how important it is for individuals to preserve their unique identities; therefore, they want the climate of the organization to be humanistic so that each person is respected for his or her personal worth and dignity.

## LEADERSHIP: PERSONALIST

The leadership style of FOURS is distinctly personal. Sensitive to peoples' feelings, they are concerned about what is personally important to individuals and about how decisions impact on people's feelings. There is a distinctly personal touch to how they appear and what their office looks like.

Before they take action and make decisions, FOURS sound out their feelings. Their conclusions may be based more on feelings than facts. Their imaginative exploration of the possibilities in ordinary situations can result in unique, creative approaches and outcomes. Intuitive in sensing genuine feelings, they can see through facades.

## THINKING STYLE: INDIVIDUALIST

FOURS are motivated by their feelings, and they personalize their thinking: They judge the value of people and things based on the extent to which they are personally meaningful. What is "true" for FOURS may depend on—and vary with—their moods. They are apt to reason more from feelings than from facts, using emotional intuition to sense others' real feelings.

## Beliefs and Principles

FOURS are able to relate to people in uniquely personal ways, valuing each person's individuality. Emotionally honest, they empathize with people who are hurting and listen to others' difficulties. They can discern uncommon possibilities in common situations and approach tasks creatively.

People of this type tend to take time with and for themselves, and tend to express themselves creatively in words, actions, and environment. Depending on their moods, they can be serious or funny.

FOURS believe that people's feelings are the human side of organizations. They perceive individual self-expression as enriching the workplace and productivity as a function of an individual's state of mind. For FOURS, the underlying principle is that people who feel that their individual identities and feelings are respected are more apt to be productive.

## Motivation and Appreciation

FOURS basically are motivated to appreciate themselves. They seek self-insight by withdrawing from people and sorting out their feelings. FOURS want to cope with their emotions, express them in creative ways, and receive special recognition. To compensate for what they miss in the real world, they are apt to fantasize or indulge themselves.

## Professional Development

FOURS develop by affirming themselves with positive statements such as "I am sensitive and imaginative." They like to renew themselves in creative ways, often artistically.

FOURS can empower their professional style in creative ways by traveling toward the life-giving ONE and by learning to manage their feelings and moods according to stable principles. An appreciation of objective standards enables FOURS to stabilize their emotional approaches to situations. With secure footing in the real world, they creatively share their emotional riches with other people, developing their work styles as Quality Performers. In addition, FOURS who are leaders become Stabilizers as well as Personalists.

Another creative way that FOURS develop their professional style is by turning to the THREE-wing or FIVE-wing. By modeling their behavior after THREES, FOURS can learn to become sociable, motivated, and achievement minded. Following in the footsteps of FIVES enables FOURS to balance intuition with logic and feelings with understanding.

## PROFESSIONAL DECLINE

In critical situations, FOURS are apt to withdraw into their feelings and fantasize about reality. If they fall into being oversensitive, they tend to feel easily hurt. When the going gets tough, they may wallow in self-pity and doubt their abilities. Their self-indulgence may lead to neglect of work, and their ideas may sound impractical to realists.

The professional styles of FOURS decline when they withdraw into themselves and become intensely absorbed in their feelings. Unfulfilled desires may result in resentment and withdrawal from others. If their emotions become numb and their thinking confused, they become very dissatisfied with themselves.

In particular, when FOURS decline toward the life-draining TWO, they cling to others and use them to get their needs met. They feel that no one understands them. Repressing their feelings and needs, they are apt to sacrifice themselves for others, giving them an excuse to wallow in sadness, tragedy, and dying. Neglectful of their own needs, they become depressed. They may turn into meddling Self-Seekers at work. Alternatively, FOURS who are leaders may become Manipulators like the unhealthy TWOS.

## PERSONAL AND PROFESSIONAL EMPOWERMENT

For personal and professional empowerment, FOURS are invited to consider the following suggestions:

- Befriend yourself by supporting, encouraging, complimenting, thanking, and affirming yourself.

- Balance empathy for others' personal problems with concern for performance standards.

- Be professionally receptive to valid, helpful criticism without becoming defensive.

- Accentuate the positive and eliminate negative self-talk.

- Be aware of the messages that feelings are relating in a particular situation. Keep in mind that feelings tell you part and not the whole of your experience.

- Use the emotional expressions of your voice and body language to communicate effectively.

- Respond objectively from your mind rather than over-reacting from your feelings.

- Commit yourself to stable standards and clear principles to guide you consistently through life's ups and downs.

- Learn to trust in a relationship that allows you to share your deepest feelings at your own pace.

- Attend to the outer world with its responsibilities, people, and tasks so as not to withdraw into the realm of fantasy.

- Allow your thinking to balance your feelings, and allow your head to balance your heart.

- Remind yourself that you have feelings but that you are not your feelings. You may have sadness but you are not sadness. You are more than what you feel.

*"The greatest happiness for the thinking man is to have fathomed the fathomable, and to quietly revere the unfathomable."*

— Johann Wolfgang von Goethe

# 7

## Enneagram Type FIVE

### Personality: Observer

FIVES are characterized as Observers. With strong tendencies for observation, they gather data, form ideas for understanding and reflection, explore possibilities, and build theories to explain situations. Constantly striving to know, they like to grasp many opinions within an all-encompassing viewpoint. As children, they learned that knowledge enables them to understand and cope with the world.

### Work Style: Thinker

FIVES are thinkers who logically analyze complex problems into simpler elements. Focusing on the inner world of ideas and theories, they strive to grasp connections between concepts. They prefer to work quietly with minimal supervision, enabling them to stay at tasks for long periods. Valuing their time, they dislike people infringing on them without clear limits. FIVES are more comfortable talking with people about ideas than feelings and may have difficulty recalling names. It is important for them to have clear ideas of what is expected.

FIVES prefer to learn alone by listening to tapes or reading books. Unclear expectations or sudden changes in responsibilities tend to drain their limited energies. Easily tired by too much pressure at work, they may withdraw until they are able to regain their strength.

In terms of organizational structure, FIVES believe that every part of the organization should fit consistently within the whole and should work systematically for the organization as a whole. They follow the economic law: Don't multiply parts without necessity.

## LEADERSHIP: SYSTEMATIZER

As leaders, FIVES tend to be Systematizers. Perceptive and insightful, they can grasp the grand ideas that enlighten people and build them into a vision to show others the way. Intellectual architects, they see an organization as a system of intelligible structures and operations.

Detached from emotions and at home in intellect, FIVES are good at planning long-range projects and making rational decisions. They are comfortable delegating authority to other people in order to accomplish a task. Therefore, at times, their tendencies to prolong reflection may keep them from taking action.

## THINKING STYLE: ANALYTICAL

The thinking of FIVES is analytical. Motivated to know, they analyze problems, observe facts, reason logically, and use charts to illustrate positions. Detached from their feelings, their thinking is seldom controlled by emotions. However, if anxiety clouds their thinking, FIVES ignore facts and impose their ideas and theories to solve a problem.

## BELIEFS AND PRINCIPLES

FIVES have a special ability to construct conceptual frameworks and to develop theories and models. They provide supporting data and systematize different ideas. The basic belief of FIVES is that organizations should be structured in order to be rationally managed; otherwise chaos and confusion might take over. People need to be aware of the vision of an organization so they understand its structure, the reason for its existence, and the direction it is going. Thus, changes can be planned for systematic development rather than being left to circumstances and chance. Their governing principle is that people with a clear understanding of an organization are apt to be productive.

FIVES value attention to data, intelligence in analyzing, consistency in connecting ideas, logical reasoning to conclusions, and factual evidence to critically validate theories and beliefs. Open-minded, they aim for profound, broad views to encompass different opinions.

## MOTIVATION AND APPRECIATION

FIVES are motivated to know as much as possible with clarity and certainty, avoiding the emptiness and insecurity that comes with ignorance. The unknown appears threatening. In the face of what is fearful, they are apt to retreat into the safety of the inner world of ideas. In addition, FIVES have strong needs to understand what is going on around them and to be sure of what is happening in an organization. When things are clear, certain, factual, and intelligible, they feel at home in their surroundings.

FIVES like to be appreciated for their insights, especially by intellectually competent people. It means a lot to them when someone listens intellectually to their ideas and theories and acknowledges their intellectual talents. They like to be complimented for their profound perception of the nature of a project or an organization. However, FIVES may be uncomfortable handing out or receiving compliments.

## PROFESSIONAL DEVELOPMENT

FIVES develop their professional strengths by affirming "I am intelligent" or "I am insightful." Believing in themselves, they can develop abilities for asking the right questions, predicting consequences, and discovering new ways of understanding traditional ideas.

FIVES can also empower themselves by journeying toward the life-giving EIGHT, functioning more from instinct than intellect. Like EIGHTS, they are confident, assertive, and express feelings appropriately. In their work styles, they are confident Thinkers, balancing knowledge with action and ideas with feelings. FIVES who are leaders can learn to be Directors in action as well as Systematizers of ideas.

Another way FIVES enhance their professional styles is by cultivating the life-giving FOUR-wing or SIX-wing. They can turn to the FOUR wing and learn to be intuitive as well as knowledgeable, sensitive as well as insightful, aesthetic as well as intellectual, personal as well as abstract. Or FIVES can model themselves after the SIX, learning to be loyal and committed to relationships and the organization.

## PROFESSIONAL DECLINE

FIVES tend to withdraw under stress. Their lack of assertiveness may keep them from social interaction and following through after the design of projects. Other people may experience FIVES as unconcerned about feelings and needs.

FIVES decline when they work from the intellect so much that they disconnect from feelings. As they withdraw from social interaction, they tend to be less effective in motivating people. They are liable to be frozen in inaction until they are certain of the world about them.

Under stress, FIVES move in the direction of the life-draining SEVEN and distract themselves in pleasure rather than dealing with problems. In this way, FIVES move more into the realm of thought, losing contact with the immediate experience, analyzing excessively, intellectualizing compulsively, and becoming fixated on details.

At work, FIVES may deteriorate into impulsive Pleasure Seekers as they decline towards the life-draining SEVEN. As leaders, they may become unrealistic visionaries like Don Quixote and joust with impractical theories. Like unhealthy SEVENS, they may become self-centered leaders, absorbed in their own ideas and thought.

# PERSONAL AND PROFESSIONAL EMPOWERMENT

For personal and professional empowerment, FIVES are invited to consider the following suggestions:

- Learn to relate to people in ways that invite them to feel comfortable with you.

- Balance the knowledge of your head with caring from your heart and assertiveness from your instinct.

- Shift your perspective from seeing conflict as a threat to your well-being to grasping it as a way of growth in relationships.

- Be open-minded and receptive to new and relevant facts to avoid leaping to conclusions.

- See reality as it actually is and accept it rather than resorting to unrealistic speculations.

- Work through disagreements to a stronger relationships rather than giving up and withdrawing from friends.

- Learn to relax your mind and body so as to balance your physical and mental energies.

- Be open to the reports of your feelings as a unique source of information about the world and how you respond to it.

- Balance observation with participation in team action.

- Express your appreciation and praise people for their work in order to motivate relationship-oriented people.

- Understand that some people find inspiration from their interactions with others.

- Learn to be centered and secure so you can share your ideas and get involved without feeling less like your own person.

*"Hold faithfulness and sincerity as first principles."*

— Confucius

# 8

# Enneagram Type SIX

## Personality: Groupist

The personalities of SIXES are described as Groupists who tend to relate in friendly and warm ways to the people close to them. They elicit endearing feelings from friends. Responsible at work, they usually respect authority and follow established customs or traditions. They are cooperative with coworkers and reliable in working on tasks. As children, they learned that belonging to a family brought them security and approval.

## Work Style: Relater

SIXES are Relaters who are cooperative with people in their groups or organizations. Just as they are reliable, SIXES want other people to be dependable at work. SIXES focus their attention on promoting trust, cooperation, and commitment to each other and the organization. When they feel secure within an organization, SIXES commit themselves to their jobs, working hard and keeping to tasks until finished. When they are given guidelines and plans, they function well.

SIXES prefer clear responsibilities and collaboration with others rather than working in confusing and competitive situations. Not given to innovation, they follow proven, reliable procedures. When tasks are complex and unfamiliar to them, they rely on the decision of authority or someone they respect. They usually get to work on time and put in a full day's work, keeping busy each moment on the job.

Cautious about being criticized, SIXES tend to communicate within a circle of trustworthy people. It is important for them to participate in the ideas and perceptions of a closely knit group. They tend to rely on authority for decisions. However, SIXES may be unsure about how to relate to authority or powerful people. They may vacillate between obedience and defiance that violates traditions and rules.

## LEADERSHIP: TEAMSTER

When their thinking coincides with the way the group or team thinks, SIXES feel secure in their leadership. To be most effective, they like a clear chain of command in which the lines of authority are distinctly drawn. For the common good, they are willing to delegate responsibility and hold others responsible. They are not apt to make decisions unless they are quite sure of themselves; for tough decisions, they may procrastinate and be uncomfortable being pressured to make quick decisions. However, once SIXES make decisions, they feel at ease.

## THINKING STYLE: GROUP MINDED

The thinking of SIXES is group-minded. Motivated to be with others they trust, SIXES base their thinking on the authority of the group as represented by other leaders, tradition, customs, or rules. They want to know what every person—or at least the majority of people—thinks about a given situation. People outside of the group or organization may be suspected of erroneous thinking. Out of fear of rejection from an organization, SIXES may suppress their individual thoughts to conform to group thinking.

## Beliefs and Principles

Once committed to an organization, SIXES expect others to be devoted to their work and to respect traditions. SIXES are reliable in fulfilling duties and cooperating with others. As team players, they tend to make people feel at home. Their work style is governed by the belief that an organization should be run according to established traditions.

SIXES are motivated by the following principle: An organization should provide a sense of belonging and an environment in which people feel safe and sure of their jobs. When people feel safe and secure, they are apt to be committed to the organization, work hard, cooperate with authority and their fellow workers, and be productive.

SIXES value the very things that they live by. They realize that people who are friendly with one another are likely to be cooperative and work as a team. They value a clear chain of command so that people know exactly where they stand on the hierarchical ladder.

## Motivation and Appreciation

The main motivation for SIXES is to feel safe and secure. To gain that security, they are willing to commit themselves to organizations and belong to groups. Getting people to like and to approve of them makes SIXES feel reassured. With people they trust, they feel safe and unafraid. They want to avoid rejection, abandonment, and insecurity.

Although SIXES may find it difficult to accept and enjoy recognition, they like to be commended for a job well done. It is important for them to be approved for their loyalty, hard work, and sense of duty. They appreciate being supported and safeguarded by friends.

## Professional Development

SIXES develop their dominant work style and leadership by self-affirmations such as "I am reliable and friendly," or "I am cooperative and loyal." By deepening their bonds with others, SIXES elicit in them stronger senses of fidelity. As they trust more in themselves and affirm themselves, they become confident and courageous as leaders.

They also empower their professional styles by journeying towards the life-giving NINE and learning to manage their fears and stabilize their emotions. As they learn to feel relaxed and secure, they become comfortable with authority and confident in their professions. Their work styles may develop into those of secure Peacemakers. SIXES who are leaders may become Reconcilers as well as Teamsters, able to help people get along and work harmoniously together.

SIXES enhance their work styles by cultivating their wings, FIVE and SEVEN. Developing the FIVE-wing helps SIXES to become knowledgeable and competent. SIXES learn from the behavior of the SEVEN-wing to be sociable, humorous, and enjoy themselves.


## PROFESSIONAL DECLINE

Under stress, SIXES may be ambivalent about authority and be lacking in inner strength to exercise authority. When they vacillate and react unpredictably, they experience uncertainty and indecision. The more anxious and insecure they feel, the more suspicious and negative they become, defending their own organizations and attacking others.

The professional style of SIXES declines when they lose faith in themselves and fear making decisions. Insecurity leads to over-relying on the authority of individuals, traditions, or organizations. Tending to be ambivalent toward authority, SIXES may behave erratically and become deceptive. They may over-react to insecure feelings by being aggressive and attacking outsiders.

At worst, SIXES regress to a low self-image and experience anxiety and cowardliness. When they decline toward the life-draining THREE, they may become frantic in their indecision and fear failure. If they feel worthless, SIXES may experience a sense of inferiority. In their work styles, they may become Exploiters. SIXES who are leaders may fall into being Opportunists—like the life-draining THREES—in order to get approval.

# PERSONAL AND PROFESSIONAL EMPOWERMENT

For personal and professional empowerment, SIXES are invited to consider the following suggestions:

- Affirm yourself with positive thinking rather than indulging in worry and insecurities.

- Respond appropriately to stress rather than exaggerating fears and aggravating the situation.

- Communicate your true thoughts and intentions by clear words and behavior.

- Take responsibility for your actions rather than allowing your anger to agitate you to blame others.

- Balance the inner authority of your mind with the outer authority of groups.

- Exercise leadership by following the middle way between obsequiousness and hostility.

- Summon up strength to face the fear of criticism and rejection and to assert yourself in appropriate ways.

- Keep one eye on technical details and the other on relationship needs.

- Develop confidence in your own abilities so you can relate appropriately to authority, accepting or questioning it as the situation requires.

- Acknowledge your anxiety and tensions as part of your inner life.

- Encourage feedback so you can manage problems before they reach critical points.

- Trust your gifts for relating to people so you can overcome fears and be willing to commit yourself.

*"Nothing great was ever achieved without enthusiasm."*

— Ralph Waldo Emerson

# 9

## Enneagram Type SEVEN

### Personality: Cheerer

SEVENS like to enjoy life and be enthusiastic. Outgoing and spontaneous, they focus on creative possibilities and reach out to people.
Gifted with various skills and interests, they do many things well. As
children, they learned that having fun makes life worthwhile.

### Work Style: Animator

As Animators, SEVENS animate others with their enthusiasm. Their
speech often is embellished with lively and imaginative words.
Sometimes they "color" the facts to make them interesting.

SEVENS prefer to be free to pursue their own interests. High in
energy, they like to explore future projects. SEVENS dislike routine
work and critical bosses. When SEVENS enjoy their work, they work
quickly and productively. However, SEVENS may find it difficult to
complete multiple tasks. If they lose interest or get wrapped up in new
ideas, they may neglect follow through. To save time or energy, they
may sacrifice quality.

SEVENS focus on the growth and satisfaction of people in organizations. They are very aware of how important it is for individuals to be happy at what they are doing. They like to see organizations alive and developing, open to innovative ideas and projects.

## LEADERSHIP: CHEERLEADER

Excited about life and its many opportunities for happiness, SEVENS like to cheer up people. They are drawn to positions that free them to pursue their own interests. They adapt easily to changing situations. Their self-assurance allows them to interact with a variety of people. However, they usually dislike confrontation and enforcing decisions.

As optimists, SEVENS promote a positive mood in a group. Although others may be discouraged, SEVENS tend to look on the bright side and anticipate positive outcomes. When the usual way of doing something is not producing results, they are ready to promote new ideas and explore alternative courses of action. In following hunches, they may jump to conclusions without sufficient reflection.

SEVENS are effective social and professional speakers. Others are influenced by their charm and vision. Socially skillful, articulate, and convinced of their own views, they can persuasively sell projects.

When they enjoy their leadership, Cheerleaders commit themselves to plan, innovate, and motivate others. However, in unpleasant circumstances, they may stall or slow down jobs, or cut corners, resulting in a lack of quality work. They dislike being bearers of bad news. Their preference is to announce good news and make people happy.

## THINKING STYLE: POSITIVE

SEVENS are positive thinkers who see possibilities rather than actualities. Motivated to be happy, they explore different ways to enjoy life and work. They are alert to possibilities unfolding out of the future. They plan events to work out for their enjoyment. However, unless their thinking is grounded in facts, it may not correspond to reality.

## Beliefs and Principles

SEVENS search for new ways to make organizations more productive. Excited about their work and responsive to situations, they keep the organization active and productive. As effective speakers, they inspire people to be optimistic in difficult times.

For SEVENS, satisfaction contributes to morale in organizations. They also believe that a positive outlook motivates people to trust in the future of an organization. SEVENS are oriented toward promoting a positive atmosphere in the workplace so that other employees will experience happiness in the organization. SEVENS follow the principle that a happy employee is likely to be a productive employee.

SEVENS value enthusiasm and spontaneity in responding to new situations. Enjoyment of their work and people is a prime value. Imaginative and versatile, SEVENS prefer new and innovative projects. They are ready to express their gratitude to people who do their jobs. Self-assured as leaders, they value the freedom to use their talents and others' abilities to accomplish tasks.

## Motivation and Appreciation

Motivation for SEVENS is enjoying life and avoiding pain. Uncomfortable with controlling impulses, they tend to do what they please. They try to avoid anxiety by always being on the go, sometimes without considering outcome.

SEVENS want to be commended for their new and innovative ideas. They also like to be appreciated for their charming manner and creative concepts. Tending to be process-minded more than product-minded, SEVENS want to enjoy themselves as they experience tasks. Of course, they welcome celebrations with others when the results are positive. SEVENS do not appreciate pessimistic people who are constantly complaining and negative.

## Professional Development

Professional style for SEVENS is developed by affirming themselves with positive statements such as "I am enthusiastic" or "I am productive." SEVENS can empower their professional style in exciting ways by journeying towards the life-giving FIVE, thereby deepening their insights into their life and work. With a profound grasp of the meaning of life and of the significance of organizations, they experience deeper appreciation for professional life. Going beyond the superficial, they become amazed at the wonders of human existence, especially the goodness of life and the spiritual dimension of reality. SEVENS who are leaders can learn from the life-giving FIVE to be profound Thinkers at work and reflective Systematizers in their leadership.

Another exciting way that SEVENS enrich their professional style is by turning to their life-giving SIX-wing or EIGHT-wing. SEVENS learn from the SIX to be loyal, reliable, and share their happiness. Following the EIGHT enables SEVENS to be more confident, assertive, and stronger in the determination to accomplish their goals.

## Professional Decline

Under stress, the professional style of SEVENS tends to decline toward the life-draining ONE, the Perfectionist: They try to plan and control the future so events will turn out to their liking and enjoyment. However, when life and work do not unfold as pleasantly as they desire, they become frustrated and angry. Fed up with trying to control their desires, they may impulsively indulge their appetites. They may fall back into the work style of life-draining ONES by becoming rigid Moralizers. SEVENS who are leaders may fall into being Perfectionists and Exhibitionists in their leadership.

With tendencies to be overactive, SEVENS are apt to become superficial and impulsive as they hop from one activity to another. If they selfishly indulge themselves, they are apt to come across to others as impatient and impolite. In their impulsive desire to get something done, they may sacrifice quality to save time.

# PERSONAL AND PROFESSIONAL EMPOWERMENT

For personal and professional empowerment, SEVENS are invited to consider the following suggestions:

- Look beyond instant gratification to discover what is good for you in the long term.

- Gain insight into experiences that are truly satisfying; it is not how much you experience, but how you experience much.

- Let your joy be unrestrained but not unrefined. You can be enjoyable without hurting another person's feelings.

- Grow in awareness of your desires, and select truly valuable interests for your fulfillment.

- Follow through on projects by patiently overcoming obstacles and consistently applying yourself to the tasks at hand.

- Be sure that you have the resources of time, money, and personnel to complete the projects you are planning.

- Look at the disadvantages as well as the advantages in planning projects so that you can see the problems, practicality, and setbacks as well as the possibilities and positive outcomes.

- Grasp what is truly beneficial, for enjoyment follows in the wake of choosing what is truly worthwhile for you.

- Listen to the good ideas and suggestions of others who can contribute to accomplishing projects.

- Exercise conscientious leadership by providing direction and structure to those who need it.

- Offer positive, constructive feedback to workers whose performances are not up to standards.

- Discover your true bliss, which lies not in satiating but in moderating desires. The result will be a balance of enthusiasm and a channeling of energy.

*"There is nothing so strong as true gentleness; and there is nothing so gentle as true strength."*

— Frances de Sales

# 10

## ENNEAGRAM TYPE EIGHT

### PERSONALITY: CHALLENGER

The personality of EIGHTS is described as Challenger. Confident and strong-minded, they assert themselves in deciding and taking action. They are natural leaders who like to take charge and get a job done. They can make tough decisions and give commands to others. Self-assured, they confront or challenge people who oppose them. As children, they learned to get what they wanted by asserting themselves.

### WORK STYLE: ASSERTER

EIGHTS are assertive in taking action; in fact, they want to take charge. Tough-minded, they can stand up to people in authority. Authority that shows signs of being unsure of itself may be tested and challenged by EIGHTS. They usually respect strong-minded leaders.

However, EIGHTS may become bored without challenging tasks. Because they prefer things their own way, they are apt to find it difficult to submit to supervision. When they start tasks, they usually finish them. It is fairly easy for them to say "no" to requests.

EIGHTS focus on power and authority in the organization. They like being in positions of authority so they can efficiently mobilize people to accomplish tasks the way they want them to be done.

## LEADERSHIP: DIRECTOR

Assertive and self-confident, EIGHTS naturally take to being leaders and directing other people. Their inner strength enables them to take on difficult challenges and tough decisions. Persuasive and forceful, they can change people's minds to their way of thinking, negotiate with firmness, and execute deals. Once they make up their minds, they hold fast to their positions, even in the face of strong opposition.

EIGHTS want to have the authority to do jobs the way they believe they should be done. When necessary, they can be tough with people to get jobs done, or they can reprimand lazy workers. They are direct and confrontive in calling unproductive and irresponsible people to task. They do not mind changing plans or procedures.

As leaders, EIGHTS want to be in complete charge of people and operations. Subordinates tend to respect their ability to give commands and make rules. Decisive, they quickly put ideas into action, once they feel sufficiently informed. Even under pressure, EIGHTS possess a presence of mind and determination to complete projects.

EIGHTS are not afraid to compete to extend their authority, sometimes targeting opponents' weaknesses. They protect allies and can rally workers to meet deadlines. The more challenging the project, the more strength they call on to finish what they start.

## THINKING STYLE: DIALECTICAL

With dialectical thinking, EIGHTS fearlessly oppose opinions of others and assertively state their own views. Knowledge is power for EIGHTS; they are more interested in putting an idea into action than contemplating it. EIGHTS may rely more on the power of their personalities than on the strength of their reasoning and evidence.

## Beliefs and Principles

EIGHTS immediately respond to problems and work efficiently to complete projects. Confident in what they do, they assert themselves and rally people to achieve goals. They are natural leaders whom other people respect and follow. Fearless, they confront reality and issues. As daring entrepreneurs, they are willing to take risks and challenge people to produce. They waste no time in making decisions.

A basic belief of EIGHTS is that an organization is no stronger than its leaders: As the leader goes, so goes the organization. If a leader is decisive, courageous, and strong, the organization will be able to survive through difficult times.

Strong leadership guarantees that things will get done. EIGHTS are motivated by the principle that when workers are accountable to a firm and assertive leader, they will be motivated to be productive. EIGHTS value strength and power. It is important for them to be self-confident and strong in asserting themselves. EIGHTS like to think of themselves as brave, willing to take risks. High in energy and assertiveness, they are forceful in putting across ideas and dynamic in putting them into action. Comfortable with authority and commanding, they can be tough-minded when it comes to making difficult decisions. Rather than waiting for circumstances to be opportune, EIGHTS take the initiative and arrange for things to happen.

## Motivation and Appreciation

EIGHTS are motivated to be self-determined and independent. They prefer to avoid domination and control by others. To be in charge, they assert themselves and try to hold sway over situations. Their will-to-power drives them to struggle for authority and leadership.

EIGHTS appreciate being independent so they can do things their own way. They also have a need to be self-sufficient so they can rely on their own resources rather than depend on other people. It is important for them to be respected for their ability to lead and exercise authority.

They like to be recognized for their fearlessness, determination, and adaptation to challenges.

## PROFESSIONAL DEVELOPMENT

Their professional style is developed by affirming themselves with positive statements such as "I am a confident and assertive person" or "I am self-determined and self-sufficient." EIGHTS also empower their professional style by journeying towards the life-giving TWO, learning to function from the heart by acquiring the power of love and by generously promoting the welfare of others. In this way, their work style takes on the altruism of the Helper. As leaders, they may become Supporters as well as Directors, balancing assertiveness with caring.

Another source of enrichment for EIGHTS is found in turning to either the SEVEN-wing or the NINE-wing. From the life-giving SEVEN-wing, EIGHTS can learn to be positive, optimistic, and enjoy life. When EIGHTS develop their life-giving NINE-wing, they learn to be calm and concerned about harmony among people.

## PROFESSIONAL DECLINE

With tendencies to be unaware of tender feelings such as compassion and gentleness, EIGHTS may become self-centered and use their power in their own self-interest to dominate other people. When they regress under stress to the life-draining FIVE, they are apt to detach further from their feelings and become aggressive and fearful of any threat to their domination. Their work style deteriorates into that of a fearful Speculator of ideas. As leaders, life-draining EIGHTS become Dictators and Visionaries with illusions of omnipotence.

EIGHTS can fall into being domineering and dictatorial. Impatient with theory and abstraction, they tend to be abrupt. If anger gets the better of them, they can be aggressive and intimidating, taking an oppositional stance and threatening others to get submission. Like Machiavelli, they act as though "might makes right."

## Personal and Professional Empowerment

For personal and professional empowerment, EIGHTS are invited to consider the following suggestions:

- Harmonize independence and self-determination with reliance on the talents of other people.

- Motivate people, not by fear of your anger, but by respect for your fairness and by trust in your caring.

- Use power reasonably and responsively, and you will gain the heartfelt respect of people.

- Build up teamwork rather than trying to accomplish too much alone.

- Empower others to assume responsibility for their lives and work so they can protect their interests.

- Balance toughness with gentleness and strength with the ability to receive help and support from others.

- Respect differences among people, and use the talents of their work styles to get results.

- Use your intellect rather than instinct to choose your battles.

- Care for power and feel the power of caring, helping, and inspiring others.

- Use the gift of assertiveness in the service of others, for it is in serving others that you will experience genuine fulfillment and joy of power.

- Balance your will-to-power by feelings of caring.

- Realize that the full meaning of power goes beyond legislating, judging, and enforcing your own interests to a larger purpose, including family relationships and God.

*"With an eye made quiet by the power of harmony, and the deep power of joy, we see into the life of things."*

— William Wordsworth

# 11

## Enneagram Type NINE

### Personality: Accepter

NINES are usually accepting, easygoing, stable, and trusting of self and others. As good mediators, they harmonize differences and make peace among conflicting parties. NINES like to think of themselves as even-tempered and peaceful. As children, they learned to find contentment by identifying with the interests and desires of others.

### Work Style: Receptionist

Receptionists welcome people and make them feel at ease. Usually calm and relaxed, they like people to get along and work in harmony. They are inclined to follow set ways of doing things. With clear directions from authority, NINES work steadily and patiently.

They usually prefer to do routine jobs with definite procedures. When they need to reduce a complex task to its simple components, they imperturbably focus on facts and move at a placid pace to a conclusion. As a rule, they are not attracted to work situations that require a lot of energy and frequent changes.

In general, NINES focus on the harmonious operation and stability of an organization. They want to see people getting along together and collaborating for peace within the organization. Obviously, NINES play a very important role because there are usually differences within an organization—different personalities, different viewpoints, different ways of communicating, and different ways of thinking.

## LEADERSHIP: RECONCILER

NINES are Reconcilers who mediate differences and settle disagreements. They usually enjoy a talent for respecting, listening, and identifying with different sides of an issue. Able to balance opposing opinions, they are usually adept at negotiating and reconciling. In their efforts to accommodate people, they may downplay objectives, or gloss over and neglect to deal with problems until they have escalated.

NINES lead by being clear about their purpose and course. Uncomfortable in ambiguous situations, they want to do what will get the job done. They are careful and exact about scheduling and making appointments. Because they are uncomfortable with confrontation, NINES may let problems reach a critical point before taking action.

## THINKING STYLE: HOLISTIC

With holistic thinking, NINES unify different parts into a whole. Their thinking plays down the differences among people and harmonizes opposing views. Their minds are able to grasp similarities amid differences in order to promote agreement and concord. For NINES, collective truth is more apt to be present when people agree.

## BELIEFS AND PRINCIPLES

Able to focus on the similarities between people, NINES can bring people together, despite differences. They are gifted with absorbing negative feelings and allowing nothing to upset them. As a result they remain poised in crisis, and calmly support other people who are troubled. They are able to receive and hold different views and opinions in their minds without upsetting their mental balance.

A basic belief of NINES is that an organization that runs smoothly will run effectively. For that to take place, people need to feel relaxed and work in harmony. When people feel at ease in an organization, they are unlikely to waste energy on disagreements and anger.

NINES like to work in a climate of peace and tranquility. In a relaxed atmosphere, it is important for them to feel self-possessed. They place a high value on equanimity and serenity. Their easy-going manners enable people to feel comfortable around them. Other people tend to perceive them as gentle and even-tempered. They prefer conventional roles which are clear and stable within an organization.

## MOTIVATION AND APPRECIATION

People of this type are motivated to live in unity with others. They find reasons for living and working with others by identifying with them. They have strong drives to maintain peace by keeping problems at a distance and patiently letting others develop in their own ways. It is important for them to avoid disagreement, discord, and disunity.

NINES like to be appreciated for their accomplishments. Recognition motivates them to put effort into their work and experience a sense of satisfaction. Because NINES tend to identify with people with whom they work, they want to get along with people and bring them together. NINES are most comfortable in situations where there are harmony and peace. They are uneasy when they are separated by disagreement from people who are important to them.

## PROFESSIONAL DEVELOPMENT

NINES develop their professional styles by affirming themselves with positive statements such as "I am relaxed and easygoing" or "I am a calm and peaceful person." The more relaxed NINES are, the more effective they are likely to be in managing conflict. Serene and content in themselves, they become more self-controlled and self-possessed.

NINES also enrich themselves by journeying towards the life-giving THREE and becoming energized and active. By becoming enthused about developing their potential and overcoming feelings of passivity and complacency, they take control of their lives and show incentive in accomplishing things. In their work styles, they may become Animators, like THREES. As leaders then, they learn to balance the calmness of the Reconciler and the enthusiasm of Motivators.

Another way that NINES can empower themselves is by cultivating their life-giving EIGHT-wing or ONE-wing. They can turn to the EIGHT-wing and learn to be assertive and strong in will. In themselves, they need to learn to balance calmness and forcefulness, power and peace. Alternatively, NINES can model themselves after the ONE by learning integrity and a desire for excellence.

## Professional Decline

NINES decline when they become too compliant and accommodating. Because they tend to be afraid of change, they retreat from conflict and gloss over problems. Their emotional laziness and lack of initiative results in apathy and procrastination. Unwilling to confront problems, they bracket out the hard realities of life and work. When their thinking becomes hazy and confused, they ruminate about idealistic ideas of harmony. Adopting stoic attitudes, NINES resign themselves to doing little or nothing to change situations.

When the talents of the NINE go to extremes, their limitations emerge. For the sake of peace, they tend to minimize the seriousness of problems. With a tendency to appease others, they can become too accommodating and too conciliatory towards others. Passive and lacking in energy, NINES may resist making necessary changes and be slow to respond to problems. In fact, they may even deny the very existence of difficulties in order to have peace at any price. Indecisiveness and procrastination may keep them from completing projects.

## Personal and Professional Empowerment

For personal and professional empowerment, NINES are invited to consider the following suggestions:

- Determine what you represent and take action to bring about whatever is important to you.

- Summon up power to manage difficulties so you can develop inner strength and be helpful to others.

- Be willing to assert yourself in a manner appropriate to effective leadership.

- Acknowledge and share your fears and dangers in relationships so they can be more meaningful.

- Find our what your priorities are, and focus your attention and energies on carrying them out.

- Attend to your breathing, acknowledging tensions in bodily sensations and observing your feelings of anger; then your mind will be one with your body.

- Summon up energy to respond to the challenges of life by directly dealing with disagreements and conflicts.

- Combine active, forceful leadership with consensus decision making.

- Have the courage to sacrifice a passing peace in order to deal with disagreements. Facing the hard reality of conflicts and working them through leads to truly fulfilling relationships.

- Be a catalyst in encouraging discussion of different views and fostering debate so valuable ideas can emerge for action.

- Be aware of whatever life-draining feelings are present in you. Inner peace begins with the recognition of conflicting feelings within.

- Be true to yourself and be your own person, and then you can be true to others.

*"And the song, from beginning to end, I found again in the heart of a friend."*

— Henry Wadsworth Longfellow

# 12

## TYPES IN RELATIONSHIPS

### INTRODUCTION

The key to successful relationships is to manage differences. It takes more than caring to make relationships work. Knowledge of different personality types empowers a person to appreciate how to interact with others. Relationship styles flow from personality type.

With knowledge of different relationship styles, you can develop successful relationships. Follow the Golden Rule: Treat others as they like to be treated. This means that people are apt to be more responsive to you and to cooperate with you when you take their preferences into account.

The experience of relationships can range from fulfilling and enjoyable to meaningless and apathetic. To people in relationships, the Enneagram offers the following insights:

■ Providing an objective framework of human relationships;

■ Recognizing the value of individual differences;

■ Identifying the strengths and the limitations of different relational styles;

■ Building understanding regarding aspects of a relationship;

- Assessing the compatibilities and tensions between people;

- Discovering and empowering personalities and their relational styles;

- Building a stable framework for emotional issues; and

- Helping people to be effective with one another in relationships.

The sections that follow describe the characteristics of each Enneagram type in terms of relationships, communication, conflict management, rapport, irritants, and avenues for growth.

# ONES

## Relationships: Moral

ONES are attracted to people who share their positive values such as honesty and responsibility. They do not like people who violate established norms of behavior. They feel comfortable in the company of punctual, stable, conventional individuals who follow accepted ways of acting. Critical people are usually kept at a distance.

ONES are usually aware of agreements about what they should or should not do in a relationship. They expect others to act responsibly by doing the right thing in the right way. Willing to help others improve, they remind them of the rules of behavior so undesirable actions can be changed.

In addition, ONES are responsive to people who correct their mistakes. Under stress, they may resort to anger as a way of controlling another person's behavior, especially if standards have been violated. They allow others to make demands on their time, as long as they are reasonable.

ONES value time as something to be used conscientiously, without wasting it. Therefore, they organize their time so as to utilize it responsibly and industriously. Time is viewed as a straight line that runs in an orderly fashion from yesterday to today to tomorrow. They are apt to feel dominated by time as an authority that dictates schedules and deadlines that they feel obligated to meet. When ONES talk less about "shoulds" and "oughts" and more about their feelings and needs, they experience greater closeness to others. They are comfortable near people who allow them to express their anger safely. Their affection is usually shown in established and customary ways at appropriate times and places. Their caring tends to be communicated in formal language.

## Communication

ONES usually communicate about what is right and correct. They speak authoritatively about what should or should not be done. Straightforward and direct, they say what is on their minds, using accurate and precise speech. Others may experience ONES as sermonizing or instructing. When angry, ONES can become argumentative.

True to their personalities, ONES tend to ask questions such as "What is the order or procedure to be followed?" "What are the guidelines or regulations?" "Is this the correct or right way to do this?" "Are we living up to our standards or ideals?"

In problem solving, ONES are quite precise in focusing on the relevant facts. They want to be sure that their approach to a given situation is correct in design. Each step is measured and thorough. To be certain their answer is right, they are apt to validate their conclusions.

## Conflict Management

ONES respond to conflict according to where they are in their own stage of development. When they are liberated from their compulsion to perfectionism, they are discerning and realistic in handling disagreements. Highly tolerant of differences, they tend to be fair and objective in resolving problems. However, when they are perfectionistic and idealistic, ONES are critical and judgmental; in their defensiveness, they are unable to accept being proven wrong.

## Rapport

ONES are attracted to people who are responsible, competent, and industrious. They like an organization to be fair and just toward its people. People who are fair with ONES and work correctly, accurately, and thoroughly are apt to get along with ONES.

## Irritants

ONES become irritated by people who do not use standard operating procedures or who disregard established rules. They can become intolerant of people whom they perceive as performing their jobs poorly. They dislike arbitrary changes of procedures and are uncomfortable dealing with controversial or opposing opinions. They can be sharply critical of people who procrastinate or do not meet deadlines.

ONES tend to irritate others by their intolerance of people with different views. They are apt to come across to others as inflexible or rigid in following rules and regulations. Others may be put off by the ONES' perfectionism and sharp tongue.

## Growth Avenues

When ONES choose to go in the direction of the life-giving SEVEN, they journey towards wholeness. They go from pessimism to optimism, and from seriousness to playfulness. They learn to acknowledge that without being perfect, they can accept themselves and enjoy life.

As ONES learn to accept themselves, they feel at home. Enlightened by faith, they sense the presence of a power beyond themselves. The realization that they participate in perfection greater than themselves can fill them with serenity. Relaxed in mind and body when they are fully alive and aware, ONES trust that the universe will unfold in an orderly way.

By learning to accept the things they cannot change in themselves and the world, ONES experience serenity. They become courageous as they progress in the things they can change. They grow by knowing that change is a gradual process that takes time and patience.

# TWOS

## Relationships: Helping

TWOS are attracted to people who make them feel wanted or loved, especially people who need their help. They tend to find their identity in how people respond to them. When others show approval or appreciation to them, TWOS feel accepted and worthwhile. It is hard for them to take rejection.

They usually like to be with people and participate in relationships. Their warm and friendly manner enables people to feel at ease with them. When TWOS feel wanted, they can be strongly committed and involved in a relationship.

Within a relationship, TWOS tend to let others be in charge and make important decisions. However, they like to influence others by giving advice and guidance. The service TWOS render tends to make people depend on them and feel obligated to them. They also may try to control others by flattery.

By attending to the needs of other people, TWOS usually gain their affection. Approval and appreciation draw them into personal relationships, and they like to be close to friends. However, they may be so caring and giving of themselves that they may be unaware or unsure of their own needs. In fact, they may even neglect their ow needs so as to please others. TWOS are inclined to believe that in relationships they give more than receive. Giving is their way of starting and maintaining a relationship.

For TWOS, time is something interpersonal. They appreciate spending time with people and making themselves available to help others in need. They give of themselves and their time to serve others. They value the time of important people. TWOS tend to view time as a circle between yesterday and today.

When situations are impersonal, time drags for them. Feeling guilty if they do not give others their time, TWOS find it difficult to say "no." In fact, they may delay getting a job done in order to spend time with people.

## Communication

TWOS communicate about the ways they can help others and resist talking about their own needs. Friendly and warm, they compliment, flatter, and advise others. They listen with empathy to the feelings of people in need. They like intimate one-to-one conversations.

TWOS are apt to ask questions such as "How does this help other people?" or "How will the employees or the boss feel about this?" or "How does this affect people's morale?"

In problem solving, TWOS focus less on the problems and more on the people who have the problems. They anticipate that by their helping, encouraging, clarifying, and advising, people will be able to solve their own problems. They believe that when people feel cared for, they are apt to be motivated to deal with their problems.

## Conflict Management

When they are fully alive and aware, TWOS handle conflict in a caring, compassionate manner; they empathize with the hurt or anger that another person may be feeling. Conflicts may arise with other people as TWOS become possessive and overbearing. Life-draining TWOS try to resolve disagreements with others by manipulating them to their own way of thinking. If that does not work, TWOS are apt to use anger and coercion to get others to agree with them.

## Rapport

TWOS are attracted to people who are in need. They like to be treated with warmth and friendliness. When TWOS are supported and encouraged by others, they tend to give more of themselves. They are at home in an organization that cares for its people. Treating TWOS in ways that they like creates rapport with them.

## Irritants

TWOS become irritated when they feel they are not being cared for as much as they care for others. It disturbs them not to be wanted for themselves or not to be appreciated for their own worth. They dislike the cold, impersonal responses of those who think only of getting the job done.

TWOS irritate others by becoming too solicitous and meddling in their affairs. Concerned about others' depending on them, they may want people to come to them for permission and advice. Others may dislike having to keep TWOS informed about everything. People do not want to be around them when they become patronizing and over-bearing.

## Growth Avenues

Growth for TWOS lies in the direction of the life-giving FOURS. Like the FOURS, TWOS need to get in touch with their feelings and needs so they can feel special. They realize they need to care for themselves and take time for themselves. Perhaps they may pursue a hobby that enables them to get in touch with culture and beauty. As they learn to express their own feelings and needs, TWOS are able to say "no" to others and "yes" to themselves.

For TWOS, freedom lies in flowing with the force of natural laws. There is an ebb and flow in the cosmos, a giving and receiving, an exhaling and inhaling, meeting others' needs and having one's needs met. They sense a power of caring beyond themselves yet something in which they participate. When TWOS realize that having their own needs met is a natural part of the cosmic process, they are freed from undue dependence on the acceptance of others.

# THREES

## Relationships: Task-Oriented

Because they are outgoing, THREES make friends easily. They mix well with people, especially those having prestige and status. They enjoy activities that enable them to present a positive public image.

THREES are attracted to relationships in which they have opportunities for achievement. When they were growing up, they probably learned that success is what counts. Consequently, they want to be effective in relationships. For example, their feelings may be expressed effectively without really being experienced inwardly.

For THREES, a relationship is more like a task to be accomplished than a way of sharing life. When career takes precedence in life, they have little time or energy for family or friends. Appearances and achievements of people may impress them more than depth of feeling.

Intimacy can be difficult for THREES who want to be seen more for what they achieve than who they are. Measuring intimacy involves doing rather than being. By doing things with others, they feel close and believe their relationships will succeed. However, when a partner is angry, THREES tend to withdraw, feeling they have failed.

For THREES, time means what works here and now. When they use time efficiently and are successful, they feel their time is worthwhile. Time is calculated to determine how much is needed to reach objectives and is viewed as a tool to achieve goals. Therefore, the value of time increases as the goals are approached.

THREES have a tendency to take on too much in too short a time. Inclined to become easily absorbed in what they are doing, they may not start or end on time. It is hard for them to take leisure time for themselves without feeling a need to do something.

## Communication

THREES talk persuasively about whatever is useful in getting results. They project a winning image to sell themselves to others. Intent on succeeding, they take every opportunity to advertise their products as well as themselves. THREES communicate assertively and energetically.

In keeping with their personality and working style, THREES ask questions that have to do with achievement, such as "What are the results or pay-offs for doing this?" or "How is this useful to realize my goals?" or "Will this work to my advantage?"

In terms of problem solving, THREES tend to see problems as goals to be achieved. They calculate practical ways to remove obstacles and decide what means will be useful to accomplish their objectives. People are motivated by THREES to take action in order to find out whether a solution works. Impatient with long intellectual discussions about issues, they want to put ideas into action to get results.

## Conflict Management

Fully alive and aware THREES are confident in their approach to conflict. Self-assured, they assert themselves in resolving disagreements in order to bring them to successful outcomes. As competition increases, THREES are apt to become tense and aggressive to avoid failure. To overcome opposition, life-draining THREES attempt to outwit others by lying or exploiting them.

## Rapport

THREES appreciate people who are self-assured and enterprising. They realize that only by believing in themselves will they be able to advance and obtain the recognition they value. It means a lot to them to be praised for their talents, ideas, and productivity. THREES are attracted to an organization that offers opportunities for promotion and prestige.

## Irritants

THREES are irritated by inefficient people and situations that offer no opportunity for promotion or advancement. They dislike rules, traditions, or biases that get in the way of maximum results. Anyone or anything suggesting failure or rejection is usually avoided.

THREES are likely to irritate others when they exaggerate to make a winning impression and come across as phony. Others dislike being taken advantage of by THREES who may even become dishonest to advance their own interests. Their attitude of superiority may alienate people.

## Growth Avenues

The journey of THREES begins with truthfulness. When THREES acknowledge who they really are, they find no need to resort to masks or prestige. They perceive their real selves as valuable apart from their accomplishments.

When they are in touch with their true selves, THREES are aware of their oneness with the universe. They realize that cosmic laws efficiently govern all things. They learn to trust the workings of the universe more than their own personal strengths. They have ceased deceiving themselves with the belief that their future depends solely on their own efforts.

When THREES develop faith in a productive power beyond themselves, they realize that results in life depend ultimately on forces beyond their own efforts. Their faith enables them to see that the cosmic laws that order the universe reflect the effectiveness and efficiency of a supreme productive power.

# FOURS

## Relationships: Approach-Withdrawal

FOURS do not mix readily with people because of their tendency to be introverted and introspective. They are attracted to people who appreciate them for their unique individuality and contribute to their self-actualization.

In relationships, FOURS tend to follow an approach-withdrawal strategy. When they feel understood by others, they draw closer to them and focus on their positive features. They enjoy imagining what it is like when they are together with others.

When FOURS are afraid of rejection and abandonment in a close relationship, they may single out negative features in a partner. Rather than risk loss of another, they withdraw to a safe emotional distance. Then, able to be objective at a distance, they are more apt to find good in the other and stabilize the relationship.

FOURS are adept at seeing others through crises and handling intense emotions. They feel deeply the joys and sadness of a relationship. When they let go of a hurtful past, they experience growth. Once secure in a relationship, FOURS share their deep feelings. They envy the good fortune of people who have hurt them.

For FOURS, time is an inner state of mind that is measured according to their moods. When they are in a negative mood, time tends to drag. While in a positive mood, they may lose track of time. Time is like a bow that tenses when they are down and loosens when they are up. Tending to become absorbed in the past, they yearn for days gone by. Time is like a circle between yesterday and today. They enjoy time the most when they are attuned to their feelings and expressing themselves creatively.

## Communication

The FOURS' style of communication flows from personality. Sensitive to their feelings, they communicate according to their moods. In positive moods, they express themselves in dramatic, happy voices. When their mood is down, FOURS speak in sad voices. They listen sympathetically to the problems of others.

FOURS are apt to ask questions such as "How can we approach this task in a creative way?" or "How does this project affect me personally and other people?" or "What is personally meaningful to me in this situation?" or "How will the decision enable people to be truly themselves?"

In terms of problem solving, FOURS are proficient in focusing on the individual and listening to find out what is troubling someone. They want to discover what is personally significant to individuals and how people feel about issues. By allowing people to express their genuine feelings, FOURS help them to think about possible solutions to problems. FOURS invite people to explore alternative possibilities so as to free their minds from fixed ideas that are not effective in solving problems.

## Conflict Management

FOURS feel at odds with themselves when they do not understand their feelings. In the face of conflict with others, FOURS who are fully alive and aware are able to disclose themselves and share their feelings in order to creatively and sensitively work toward solutions. However, life-draining FOURS are apt to withdraw into themselves and fantasize in order to avoid conflict and the hard realities of life.

## Rapport

FOURS get along with people who are sensitive and emotionally honest in expressing their feelings. They are attracted to an organization that awards them special recognition for being unique and making distinctive contributions. They feel comfortable with people who commend them for their grace and flair. Able to see through a facade, FOURS like people who are authentic.

## Irritants

FOURS are irritated by people who are insensitive to others' feelings or who do not respect individuality. An impersonal system that disregards a person's feelings is unattractive to FOURS. They dislike being treated as ordinary and average.

FOURS can irritate others by moodiness and changing feelings. When melancholic, they tend to be unapproachable. Others may find it difficult to know whether to approach FOURS who are unpredictable and emotionally up and down. Absorbed in their feelings and imagination, FOURS may have unrealistic expectations of others.

## Growth Avenues

FOURS advance in their journey by going towards the life-giving ONE. Like the ONE, they need to face reality and take action rather than stay in depression. By reclaiming their own strength, goodness, and talents, they can affirm "I like myself as I am," without exaggerating their feelings.

As FOURS come into harmony with their environment, they experience equanimity. Their response to situations is not exaggerated but measured and moderated. Balanced in feelings, FOURS are happy in the present. They accept themselves and envy no one. Awakened to their connection with the cosmos, FOURS realize that birth and life are governed by cosmic laws. Conscious of a source beyond themselves, they sense something special about themselves in the present. They accept themselves as unique participants in the cosmos.

# FIVES

## Relationships: Intellectual

Because FIVES tend to focus on ideas and thoughts, they do not usually initiate relationships with people. However, they are attracted to people who take the time to enter their world of ideas and dialogue with them about theories and the nature of organizations. Because they are so knowledgeable, they may be selective in finding someone with whom they are comfortable discussing abstract ideas. However, they may become defensive when their ideas are criticized.

FIVES tend to be ambivalent in their relationships with other people. On the one hand, they are curious enough to observe people and events; on the other hand, they become detached as they retreat into the realm of concepts for understanding. They are comfortable with people who allow them adequate time and space to reflect and restore their energies.

Once in a relationship, FIVES can withdraw emotionally in the face of anger from others: Intense emotions drain their energies. In such situations, they dissociate from their feelings. Alone, they review emotional encounters to understand what happened. Therefore, other people often perceive FIVES as withdrawn and aloof; it takes time to get to know them. Even their friends may find it hard to know what they are feeling, because they are not emotionally expressive.

For FIVES, time tends to be impersonal and abstract. When they get wrapped up in concentration on a project, they lose track of time. This does not mean they are unaware of time. FIVES plan their time step-by-step by proportioning it rationally to tasks and fairly to persons. As they observe and precisely parcel out their time, they like to intelligently connect the past, present, and future into a meaningful whole. It is important for them to be thorough and productive in their use of time.

Their devotion to intellectual pursuits may lead to their neglect of leisure time. They never seem to have enough time to know everything they want to know. Miserly with their time, they have little or no time to deal with the priorities of other people.

## Communication

The contents of the FIVES' communication are ideas and theories. They are adept at clearly summarizing long discourses and fitting everything together into a coherent view. Their words are economically chosen so as not to be embarrassed by saying something foolish. Rather than get lost in details, they focus on the essential ideas. They generalize from particular cases to make abstract statements. FIVES like to explain things by connecting parts into a meaningful whole.

With a strong intellectual bent, FIVES tend to ask questions such as "What reasons are there to warrant that opinion?" or "Does that conclusion logically follow from the premises?" or "What strategy is required to resolve that issue?" or "How can we be certain these ideas adequately explain the problem?"

In terms of problem solving, FIVES approach problems in very methodical ways by observing data, exploring new theories, analyzing ideas for clarity, interpreting situations in the light of their ideas, seeing whether facts confirm or disconfirm their views, and predicting consequences of their ideas in action. Their strength lies in investigating theoretical or speculative questions.

## Conflict Management

FIVES are apt to experience conflict when others frustrate their efforts to understand things. Fully alive and aware FIVES handle disagreements by dissociating their thinking from their feelings, observing how others are behaving, and analyzing what is going on between themselves and their adversaries. Life-draining FIVES, however, react to conflict by withdrawing from the source of stress, shutting down feelings, and isolating themselves from others.

## Rapport

FIVES like people who are intellectually alert and intelligent in analyzing situations logically and objectively. They like to discuss theories and ideas, and synthesize them into a grand world-view. They prefer to investigate the theory that underlies an organization or a project. It means a lot to FIVES when others understand and recognize their ideas. They are comfortable with other people who communicate clearly and rationally. An organization that offers them an opportunity to increase their knowledge or share their expertise with others is appealing to them.

## Irritants

FIVES are uncomfortable with people who violate the rules of logical reasoning. They quickly shut off unreasonable people who talk irrationally. Because they tend to be out of contact with their own feelings, they are ill at ease with emotional individuals whose thinking is confused and unclear. Discussion of superficial issues is unappealing to them, and sudden changes in responsibilities or schedules can disturb them. They dislike people who infringe on their time or have unrealistic expectations of them.

FIVES irritate other people by their excessive analyses and explanations. Unexpressive with their feelings, they tend to come across as cool and aloof, and hard to read.

## Growth Avenues

The awakening of FIVES occurs as they learn that living is more than knowing, and as they accept their ignorance of many things. Wisdom for Socrates, an ancient Greek philosopher, lay in knowing that he did not know, an awareness of the limitations of human knowledge.

When FIVES become aware of their connection with the cosmos, they realize that their mind and body are governed by laws in the universe, and they see the illusion of escaping into a world of ideas. Real knowledge comes not from being a spectator but a participant, involved in events and interacting with people.

When FIVES realize they do not have to know everything in order to live, they experience freedom from their compulsion to know. They are disposed to trust divine providence and the universal reason of the cosmos. Faith in an infinite intelligence knowing and governing the world helps FIVES to let go of their addiction to knowing.

# SIXES

## Relationships: Loyal

Although SIXES tend to be reserved and introverted, they want to be in relationships. However, they do not associate with just anyone; trust is necessary. When they are convinced of another's trustworthiness and reliability, they feel secure, manage their doubts, pledge their fidelity, and express their affection in warm and friendly ways.

SIXES may be ambivalent about assuming authority in a relationship. As long as they feel someone can be trusted, they are willing to let that person assume responsibility and make decisions. However, if they doubt that person's commitment or loyalty, fear motivates them to take control, structure activities rigidly, and revert to customs or duty to back up their positions.

By giving in relationships, SIXES develop closeness. They support and aim to please their partners. Safe and secure in giving, they feel sure of being loved. Giving enables them to have control over the state of the relationship, whereas receiving makes them feel uncomfortably dependent on another person to satisfy their needs.

When SIXES are hurt or angry, they are apt to withdraw to a safe distance. If they feel safe enough to talk through an issue, they feel better about the relationship. They feel reassured when another person affirms his/her faithfulness and affection.

In terms of time, SIXES tend to feel controlled by it. They work fast and hard to keep deadlines. Wanting to be reliable, they are punctual in arriving and leaving. Because SIXES value time within an organization, they believe their time is well spent when they are responsible in fulfilling their duties. However, feeling pressured by time, they are apt to place demands on other people to get things done on time.

## Communication

In their communication, SIXES focus on duties and traditions. They are careful in their speech to be sure that what they say agrees with the customs and norms of the group. Aware of the limits of an organization, they hesitate to criticize its established norms. SIXES speak and listen in friendly ways to the people within their group, but their communication with people outside is cautious.

SIXES are apt to ask questions such as "What are your duties or responsibilities?" or "Who can we count on to work hard in the organization?" or "What are the traditions or established ways of doing things in the organization?"

People of this type promote a team effort to solve problems. They want to find out what the group sees as the problem and how the group prefers to approach an issue. They will appeal to long-standing and established methods for resolving difficulties. Whatever the group considers to be relevant data is acceptable to SIXES. It is difficult for them to offer alternative solutions that are not in accord with the group mind.

## Conflict Management

Stress for SIXES occurs when their security is threatened or others disapprove of them. Fully alive and aware SIXES respond to conflict by cooperating with others, trusting them, and working responsibly to bring about conciliation. Insecure SIXES tend to appeal to authority and tradition to settle differences. Life-draining SIXES become defensive in the face of disagreements, blame others for difficulties, and put themselves down.

## Rapport

SIXES are attracted to people who are committed to the organization, those who are loyal and dependable, and those who are friendly and industrious workers. They are attracted to an organization that has a clear chain of command from the top leadership down to the lowest person on the hierarchical ladder.

## Irritants

In situations in which they feel rejected or left alone, SIXES become disturbed. They are irritated with people who are unreliable at work, disrespectful of traditions, uncooperative with others, and disloyal to the organization. When situations are ambiguous and their authority is unclear, they are uncomfortable. In addition, it is difficult for them to take criticism from someone in authority.

When SIXES are unsure of themselves and give contradictory signals about what they want, they irritate others. The more cautious they become, the more they procrastinate. To compensate for insecurities and show that they are their own masters, SIXES may assume a tough stance. Their reaction to perceived threats is to become defensive and blame others who do not belong to the inside group.

## Growth Avenues

Cautious SIXES grow when they journey towards the life-giving NINE's calm disposition. In touch with their instincts, SIXES listen to their own inner authority, articulating their own needs and intuitions. In contact with their inner beings, SIXES experience courage in the face of fears and choose to be true to themselves.

In touch with their own inner authority, SIXES feel secure in the realization that they are members of the cosmic community and belong to a power greater than themselves. Cosmic laws are seen as expressions of a universal authority, and fear and doubt are perceived as the results of perceiving the world as hostile.

# SEVENS

## Relationships: Social

Outgoing and gregarious, SEVENS make friends easily. They are attracted to people who are lively, active, and enjoyable company. People who are pessimistic, emotionally needy, or complaining a lot, do not appeal to SEVENS. Usually ready for a good laugh, they prefer an environment that is alive with activity or fun. SEVENS are willing to commit to relationships as long as they feel free to pursue their interests and adventures. Feelings of boredom are managed by participating in exciting and various experiences.

Intimacy is developed for SEVENS both by controlling unpleasant interactions and by sharing positive, enjoyable experiences. Although they find it hard to confront critical partners, they can be relied on for encouragement in difficult times. Their positive outlook brightens the darker moments of any relationship.

For SEVENS, time is expansive against the unlimited horizons of a future with infinite possibilities. They anticipate and plan so projects will work satisfactorily. Hopeful about the future, they are interested in fresh ideas and enthusiastic about actualizing projects. However, SEVENS may have trouble being on time, especially when the present situation is inconvenient, such as having to deal with unpleasant or routine details. They tend to procrastinate in the face of difficulties. Although they generate many ideas and dabble in different projects, they can be slow to put those ideas into action and implement projects.

## Communication

Enthused about life, SEVENS like to talk about anything that is pleasant and enjoyable. They are easily given to gossip. Responsive to people, they enjoy telling stories and talking in lively language to entertain others. Their light, humorous style of speaking makes them good masters-of-ceremony. SEVENS especially like to describe events in a positive light.

They are apt to ask questions such as "How can we be satisfied and enjoy our work?" or "What do we need to do to assure positive results?" or "How can we approach this task in a new and different way so as to get the outcomes we want?" or "What new and interesting ideas need to be explored?" They ask questions about many different things and possibilities.

In problem solving, SEVENS generate interest and enthusiasm. Impatient with routine issues, they like to tackle new and challenging problems. Rather than offer traditional responses, they prefer to explore innovative approaches and participate in exciting brainstorming for new ideas and solutions.

## Conflict Management

When others impede their happiness, SEVENS experience conflict. Life-giving SEVENS respond to conflict by looking for solutions enthusiastically and utilizing their varied talents to come to positive outcomes. They willingly collaborate with others to achieve reconciliation. When attempts to manage conflict increase their dissatisfaction, life-draining SEVENS are likely to avoid stressful situations, become uncooperative, and impulsively indulge their own wants.

## Rapport

SEVENS appreciate people who are innovative, sociable, and optimistic. They like workers to be energetic and multi-talented so they can adapt to different activities and do jobs quickly. They get along well with people who are talented and enjoy doing a variety of things.

## Irritants

Routine work and unstimulating organizations bore SEVENS, and critical bosses irritate them. They dislike being around people who are usually pessimistic or do not give them positive feedback. With their tendencies to get distracted, SEVENS' perpetual motion and frequent, loud talking can irritate others.

## Growth Avenues

Growth for SEVENS occurs when they journey toward the life-giving FIVE. When SEVENS learn, like the FIVES, to be detached from immediate gratification, they become serious about following through in their work rather than flitting from interest to interest. With the thorough, methodical approach of a FIVE, SEVENS are more apt to integrate their plans, focus on goals, and move into action.

Fully alive and aware SEVENS find that a sober attitude toward life leads to balance. Rather than indulge in unbridled activities, multiple projects, and endless future planning, they moderate their behavior. They proportion their energy and action according to the law of economy: Don't multiply activities without necessity. By living in the present, SEVENS find happiness by advancing moment by moment at a consistent pace.

As they progress spiritually, SEVENS develop a consciousness of the present, an awareness of reality as a uniform succession of "now." The wonder of the cosmos can be experienced as a constant unfolding of the here-and-now, living and working in the moment rather than looking to future accomplishments or escaping from currently unpleasant experiences.

# EIGHTS

## Relationships: Challenging

Outgoing and gregarious, EIGHTS like to be with people who will participate in activities they themselves enjoy doing. Although they may feel that people are not really interested in them personally, they nonetheless are assertive and forceful in getting their attention. EIGHTS may be direct and blunt to get people's attention, sometimes to the embarrassment of others. To relate in the ways they prefer, EIGHTS may ignore social conventions.

Afraid of being dominated, EIGHTS want to be in charge of relationships. When in control, they are confident of getting their own way and making their own decisions. It is important for them to feel that they have sufficient power over their own interests. As long as EIGHTS keep their guard up and present a strong stance, they feel safe and secure. Only after they trust a person will they let their defenses down. However, submissive individuals are apt to bore EIGHTS.

EIGHTS respect people who are strong and fair with them. Those who have them as friends or allies enjoy good protectors and powerful defenders. In arguments, they are forceful opponents. EIGHTS usually avoid close ties lest they become vulnerable and expose their weaknesses. Fearful of sharing feelings of tenderness and affection, they prefer to keep a safe emotional distance from others. Not until they can be really sure of another's trust will they entrust their personal concerns and needs. However, they do not hesitate to express tough feelings, such as anger. By being superficially friendly to people and by dominating close relationships, EIGHTS maintain comfortable roles for themselves.

For EIGHTS, time is controllable, and they adapt the clock by measuring time according to their own interests. They are impatient with limits set by other peoples' time: Their present is the important time. Time means now when EIGHTS are in action.

## Communication

EIGHTS communicate about what strength and power can accomplish. Blunt and direct, they do not hesitate to say what is on their minds. Their communication is forceful and assertive, and they debunk what they dislike or do not understand. Commands or prohibitions come naturally in their conversations, and their voices usually convey strength and confidence.

In keeping with this forceful style, EIGHTS ask questions such as "Whose in charge?" or "How much authority do I have?" or "Who controls this operation?" or "How soon can we start and finish?"

For problem solving, EIGHTS begin by determining what is a problem and what is not a problem. They have little patience for reflecting on ideas or possible solutions; they want to find out what will work. Therefore, they put ideas into action to test which solutions work and which do not. When impasses are reached, EIGHTS assert their authority in order to keep the pace on track to advance toward resolution.

## Conflict Management

EIGHTS experience conflict when other people attempt to control or dominate them. Fully alive and aware EIGHTS respond by confidently asserting themselves, collaborating with others, and decisively working towards a solution. Life-draining EIGHTS react to conflict by forcefully confronting their opponents and attempting to impose their will on others. They may become aggressive, threatening, and vindictive in enforcing their will.

## Rapport

Predictably, EIGHTS get along with people like themselves who are assertive and self-confident risk takers. They pride themselves on self-determination and tough-minded approaches, and they want others to respect them for their boldness and power to lead.

## Irritants

EIGHTS get irritated when others try to dominate them. They resent any restrictions placed on them and get irritated at being told how to work or at not being respected for their authority. Likewise, EIGHTS irritate others by their aggressiveness and sometimes intimidating ways. Their tendencies to take the opposite position in whatever is stated makes others impatient with them. In addition, when EIGHTS discover another person's weakness, they do not hesitate to criticize.

## Growth Avenues

EIGHTS advance on their journey when they move from an oppositional to a gentle response to life, from attacking the world as threatening to responding to people as good and trustworthy. This change does not mean that EIGHTS turn from tigers to kittens. Their transpersonal development lies in balancing toughness and tenderness. As EIGHTS develop their tender sides, they become helpful in giving of their time and energy for the good of others.

Underlying the life-giving EIGHTS' attitude of gentle strength is a new way of thinking about the universe. They see themselves as participating in the cosmic laws that inexorably bring about justice in the natural unfolding of events. Everything in heaven and on earth has its appointed time. EIGHTS realize that the universe takes care of itself and its own. Personal redress is not always necessary. For that reason, they do not have to be all-controlling or right all injustices.

# NINES

## Relationships: Accommodating

NINES are attracted to people with whom they can identify. Because they tend to spontaneously accept people and welcome them without judging, NINES make people feel at home. If they over-identify with persons, they may be confused about their own individuality. If they become enmeshed with others and mirror the others' aspects, NINES do not discover sufficiently who they are themselves. In such situations, they may be possessive or overdependent.

In relationships, NINES do not dominate others. On the contrary, they are usually accommodating, willing to put others' interests first. Although NINES are compliant in following the decisions of others, they may blame those people for unfavorable consequences. Although outwardly agreeable, NINES may question commitment and resist giving themselves completely to an organization. Although obliging, NINES still want their views and opinions to be heard.

Because NINES tend to identify with others, they may find a partner's mind clearer than their own ideas. In fact, they may even surrender their own way of thinking to please other people. As a result, their personal awareness of their own views and needs becomes lessened. If they acquiesce too much, NINES may resent being controlled by the decisions of others. When they feel manipulated, they are apt to become uncooperative and look for other outside interests. NINES may need to examine whether or not their own passive and pliant behavior invites others to dominate them.

For NINES, caring means merging their thoughts and feelings with those of others. Experiencing intimate friends as parts of themselves, they assume their friends' interests as their own. Ideally, they desire to be as close as they can to friends. In fact, friends may become their reason for living and working. For this reason, relationship breakups are very hard for NINES; it is like letting go of a part of themselves. Consequently, in relationships, NINES struggle to preserve their own individuality as they move closer.

NINES experience time as an even, steady movement from past to present to future. Each moment tends to have the same duration, and each event seems to have the same significance. Once they set and fill their schedules, NINES like to persist in their work. They are usually uncomfortable with too many demands placed on them within a period of time, and intensely emotional times can easily disturb them. Preferring the status quo, they get unsettled with changes in schedule. Therefore, once things are set, they dislike new things being added.

## Communication

In conversations, NINES prefer to talk about what is not controversial and provocative. Easygoing, they speak with soft, calming voices. Their relaxed, matter-of-fact style of communicating makes others feel at ease around them. Not given to emphasizing significant matters, their speech tends to be monotone.

NINES ask questions such as "How can disagreements be resolved?" or "What is the source of the conflict?" or "How can we get people to work together?"

In problem solving, NINES tend to be calm. They like to follow set procedures in figuring out what to do about problem and how to understand them. They are open to different ideas and to alternative solutions that may be diametrically opposed. In particular, NINES have a facility to motivate people to agree on solutions. Their ability to remain calm when others' tempers flare has a calming effect on people. Although they themselves may hesitate to make final decisions, they help people with different views come to consensus.

## Conflict Management

NINES experience conflict when their desires for union with others and harmony are frustrated. Fully alive and aware NINES respond with equanimity in dealing with others, patiently listening to complaints, and calmly collaborating with others. Less life-giving NINES are apt to be accommodating in handling disagreements and to minimize problems to appease others. Life-draining NINES repress conflicting feelings and passively ignore or deny problems in order to have peace at any cost.

## Rapport

It is important for NINES to receive support and attention from people with whom they identify, at work and in life. Therefore, NINES like peacemakers and patient people, preferring those who are easy to get along with and emotionally stable.

## Irritants

NINES dislike being put under pressure in tense situations, and they are irritated by people who are quarrelsome and contentious. Preferring to stay clear of rebellious individuals who provoke conflict and friction between people, they get uneasy with frequent changes in procedures.

Their indecision and procrastination in the face of difficulties irritates others. The NINES' lack of response to critical situations or their avoidance of problems frustrates those around them. Followers can lose faith in the leadership of NINES when they avoid difficulties and conflict.

## Growth Avenues

NINES grow when they learn, like the life-giving THREE, to be active and energetic, efficient and successful. Like THREES, they need to take action in dealing with problems and feeling useful as members of a team or organization. Aware of their own inner power and competence, NINES act effectively in resolving difficulties.

Quality deepens for NINES when they awaken to the purpose of life. They begin to realize that all life is motivated by an attracting power such as love or spirit, which gives meaning to all vital activity. Animated by an inner force or energy, NINES overcome a tendency to indolence and no longer feel separate from the world but somehow one with it. Aware that a cosmic spirit or power has breathed life into them, NINES feel worthwhile and lovable in themselves. They are thankful for the gift of life which they have received, and they experience reality as a harmony of opposites.

*"We weave the tapestry of life with colors all our own."*

— John Greenleaf Whittier

# 13

## ENNEAGRAM AND COLORS

### PERFECTERS AND WHITE

The color of ONES is white. White symbolizes what is bright, clear, and untarnished. ONES prefer a clear conscience and a clean heart. They like to see themselves as right and good. Whereas black is the "No" to conscience, white is the "Yes." White suggests a sense of deliberation, in which ONES' natural impulses and emotions are carefully managed. It is important for ONES to have a clean slate in their moral lives. Dark dealings are avoided so that ONES can maintain a good reputation. White indicates a concern for honesty and integrity in their work.

### CARERS AND PINK

Pink represents Carers. Pink is a light red color that aptly describes the warmhearted, friendly, gentle concern of TWOS for people in need. Whereas red corresponds to tough-mindedness, pink refers to tender heartedness. The intense, vital force of red is softened to become an empathic energy that extends a helping hand to others and evokes a desire for an intimate life. Pink corresponds to love and affection, to an interest in and a desire for relationships, but with a fervor more managed than the ardor of red. In the pink, caring TWOS reach out to support and help fellow workers.

## ACHIEVERS AND GREEN

Achievers are symbolized by green, the universal color of nature, the color of life and vitality, productivity and plenty; this is especially appropriate for THREES, who assert themselves and persist with tenacity to get results. Green suggests people who want to impress others and get recognition by advancing in their socioeconomic standings or positions. Events are managed and directed to obtain desired outcomes. Green also indicates people who value self-affirmation highly and who stand as proudly as the majestic sequoia.

## CREATORS AND PURPLE

The uniqueness of Creators is represented by purple, which suggests profound feelings that can range from the heights of joy to the depths of tragedy. Purple, a mixture of red and blue, unifies the impulsive conquest of red and the gentle surrender of blue, leading to sensitive feelings and a special self-identity among mortals. A world of imagination and creativity emerges. As a result, the FOUR experiences a unique glamor that fascinates others. Purple represents an intuitive and aesthetic appreciation, a sentimental and sympathetic outlook on life. At once introspective and temperamental, artists are often FOURS, whose fine sense picks up the subtle and sublime that can go unnoticed by others. It is a distinctly purple trait of FOURS to be grief stricken and indignant at the sufferings and misfortunes of humanity.

## OBSERVERS AND GRAY

Gray is the color of Observers who value the "gray matter" of the brain that empowers them to think and understand the world. As a neutral color, gray suggests the unemotional detachment and noninvolvement of FIVES, even when they are in relationships. They see the various nuances or shades of gray in discussions at work. Like gray, their cautious thinking compromises between great extremes. Gray represents the FIVES' turning away from excitement and emotions to steady and sure knowledge. As gray is the quiet mixture of the entire spectrum, so the thinking mind of FIVES aims to know everything it can. It corresponds to the FIVES' living on an even keel, moderately in the middle between ecstasy and despair.

## GROUPISTS AND BROWN

Brown, the earthy color, always present, is the symbol of SIXES, who are committed, reliable, and faithful. It is the color that places importance on "roots": hearth, home, companionship, and the security of belonging. Brown suggests the SIXES' need for safety and ease in familial surroundings and a desire for release from feelings of insecurity. It goes with sound and dependable people. SIXES are loyal to the group to which they belong. Brown symbolizes SIXES because of their faithful performance of duty, industry, and dedication to commitments and responsibilities at home and work. The traditional character of SIXES is represented by brown, which connotes an ageless quality. Their views are definite, and their thinking is sure and steady.

## CHEERERS AND YELLOW

Cheerers are represented by yellow, the brightest color, radiating like the warm sunlight and aglow like gold. Yellow symbolizes SEVENS with their activity, spontaneity, expansive personalities, desire for new projects, changing interests, original thinking, exhilaration for life, hope and expectation of greater happiness, whirlwind of industry, desired release from existing difficulties, and freedom from restrictions. Their positive and hopeful attitude naturally looks to the future and better possibilities in relationships and at work, Yellow, like SEVENS, presses forward, toward the new, the modern, the developing, and the unformed. Yellow suggest the SEVENS' penchant for change, sometimes just for the sake of change, and an eager quest for a variety of experiences. Yellow is never at rest, stretching ever outward in its pursuits of new adventures.

## CHALLENGERS AND RED

Red symbolizes Challengers, their strength of will and desire, their passion and excitement. Like fiery Red, EIGHTS are intense in feeling and emotionally expressive in relationships. Red connotes the EIGHTS' high energy, which is usually directed outward, articulated in quickly formed opinions, and acted out with assertiveness and power. Active and autonomous in nature, EIGHTS boldly stand out, like red, in their strong desires to compete, conquer, dominate, and lead at work. Afire like red, they are compelled to act in the present and to control events, which they shape to suit themselves. Red expresses the EIGHTS' vital force and instincts to take action and to win.

## ACCEPTERS AND BLUE

Blue is a calming color that applies aptly to Accepters, who are quiet in temperament, unflappable in their composure, and careful in their deliberation. Conservative, like blue, NINES are cautious in words and action, secure in their hold on impulsive emotions, and steady in character. Blue suggests peacefulness, which comes across in the NINES' set opinions and beliefs, tolerance of diverse individuals, relaxation and contentment in most situations, easygoing manner in relationships, tranquil appearance, and patience and perseverance at work. NINES are attracted to a tension-free environment in which events develop smoothly and relationships are free from contention. Blue represents the NINES' yearning for the harmony of differences.

*"To tend, unfailingly, unflinchingly, towards a goal, is the secret of success. But success? What exactly is success? For me it is to be found not in applause, but in the satisfaction of feeling that one is realizing one's ideal."*

— Anna Pavlova

# 14

# APPLICATIONS OF THE ENNEAGRAM

## STUDYING ENNEAGRAM TYPES

A study of the Enneagram system helps to build personal awareness and improve communication in all aspects of life. The better a person understands himself or herself, the better the chances that that person will be able to understand others and how best to interact with them.

### The Enneagram Inventory and Profile®

One of the best ways to achieve a deeper understanding is to use The Enneagram Inventory and Profile®. This 72-item self-assessment allows a person to determine not only his or her dominant Enneagram type, but also those subtypes that have significant effects for that particular person. In other words, in addition to a dominant type and arrows and wings of development, a person might also be influenced by one or more strong subtypes. Information about ordering the inventory is listed at the end of this chapter.

# Training Applications

The Enneagram lends itself to a variety of business applications. The sections that follow outline just a sample of the ways that the Enneagram can be used in organizational settings to improve productivity.

## Developing Interpersonal Style

The morale of an organization or community depends on how well people relate to one another. People tend to relate to others in familiar ways. Working out of their own experience, they tend to like other people to relate to them in comfortable ways. For example, people who like to talk about ideas and theories are attracted to people who talk about ideas and theories.

However, it is fallacious to reason that because one person likes to hear about ideas and theories, other people have the same preferences. They may or may not appreciate discussing ideas and theories, depending on their personalities and how they relate to others.

The Golden Rule states, "Do unto others as you would have them do unto you." There are two important psychological implications in that statement: (1) that a person should do well to himself or herself, and (2) how to do that. The Golden Rule includes both aspects of doing well for self and others. But can a person correctly assume that what is good for self is also good for others?

How some people treat themselves or love themselves may be different from how others treat themselves and love themselves. How other people love themselves depends on who they are, their personality, their character, their ways of thinking and feeling, their motivation and self-perception.

The Golden Rule prescribes an individual to love others in ways that are meaningful to them, something of value to the way they think, feel, communicate, cope, and are motivated. Knowing the traits and characteristics of others enables a person to understand how they want to be treated.

Understanding people's personality types and professional styles puts an individual in an advantageous position. A person who knows what others appreciate and do not appreciate, who relates to others in ways that they like, and who treats others in the ways they want to be treated, generates trust and cooperation in those other people.

## Enhancing Rapport

Rapport develops when people find out what they have in common. According to an ancient saying, "Like likes like" (Simile simili gaudet). A person tends to be attracted to people like themselves and uncomfortable with people who are different. For example, people of the same race, religion, and age tend to associate with one another.

It is obvious that people in relationships have many other similarities and differences. Rapport tends to improve as similarities increase, but when there are too many similarities, the curve of rapport may level off because of a lack of challenge and interest. Yet there is some truth in the familiar saying that opposites attract. For example, an introvert and extrovert may be drawn to each other because each offers to the other something that he or she does not have but would like to experience. An introvert may enjoy the social activity and excitement of the extrovert, and the extrovert may find it relaxing and strengthening to be with an introvert.

As much as similarities may be the foundation of a relationship, differences develop it. With sufficient similarities, people can enjoy sharing what they have in common. On the basis of that commonality, they can enrich their lives by learning new and challenging things from each other.

Rapport is enhanced by reflecting and matching similarities and differences. In matching, a person adjusts his or her responses to another person's, reflecting or mirroring it. When someone matches and reflects another's behavior and words, the two bond, almost as if they were bonding with themselves. For rapport, mirroring words are only 7% effective, compared to 93% effectiveness of voice and body.

Matching similarities may be natural and spontaneous. However, matching what is different and unique about other people requires observation of their behavior: the tone, tempo, pitch, and volume of voice, as well as posture, breathing, gestures, touching, facial expressions, eye contact, and nearness or distance in space.

By approximating another person's behavior, an individual tends to experience events in similar ways. For example, a person who is dealing with a ONE might try using the self-talk of a ONE ("I am a correct person" and "I am neat and well-groomed"). Then, by matching and reflecting the ONE's style of behaving and speaking (precise and careful speech, even tempo, moderate volume, constant pace, direct eye contact, firm handshake, controlled gestures, erect posture, appropriate distance, and so on), the two experience rapport.

## Team Analysis and Cooperation

People interact with one another in groups in terms of similarities and differences. Although members of a team may feel comfortable with people like themselves, they can be enriched by relating to people with different talents and gifts. In addition, a team usually requires different abilities for different functions.

The key is to integrate different personalities and different professional styles into a cohesive whole so the team can efficiently achieve its objectives. Otherwise, the differences are apt to result in recurring disagreement and conflict, thereby draining the team of its energy and subverting its effectiveness.

## Creative Team Problem Solving

The aim of team development is to identify and improve the individual styles of problem solving so the team can be effective in doing its job. Collaboration among team members for effective problem solving requires an appreciation of one another's styles of communication, conflict management, cooperation, and so on.

No one way of solving problems applies equally well to all situations. Some situations require critical thinking and standard procedures; others require affective thinking, which operates more from the heart (feelings) than from the head (reasoning). The needs of the situation dictate the specific problem-solving response. The end result is always enhanced by collaborative efforts and focused energies.

## FOR MORE INFORMATION

Training programs on these topics and others, all of which are based on The Enneagram Inventory and Profile® are available from:

Pfeiffer

An Imprint of Jossey-Bass Inc., Publishers

350 Sansome Street, Fifth Floor

San Francisco, California 94104

415-433-1740 or 800-274-4434

*"It is good to have an end to journey towards; but it is the journey that matters, in the end."*

— Ursula K. LeGuin

# 15

## FUTURE DIRECTIONS

### EMPOWERMENT

Learning more about the Enneagram is an unfolding process. It begins by experiencing, and continues on to insights, affirmations, and choices. By passing through these stages, a person's authentic self emerges.

### PERSONAL AND PROFESSIONAL STYLE

The elements of experience, insight, and affirmation find their fulfillment in the choices a person makes. Through real-life experiences, a person gets input and information from the world. Insight and affirmation enable a person to process and know about these experiences. The sections that follow describe ways to enhance the Enneagram experience and its applications to personal and professional life.

#### Being Motivated

Motivation is an essential characteristic self. A person cannot be true to his or her deepest nature without needing or desiring something of value. Clarity of motivation is essential for life-giving choices in life and work. A person who is clear about his or her purpose in life and goal at work is ready to commit to achieving that objective.

Motivation consists of mission and fulfillment. A mission embraces the values of person, and task aims to fulfill those values. Therefore, people are drawn by three motivators: serving people, achieving tasks, and being fulfilled—or Caring, Achieving, or Fulfilling.

## Potentialities

Two basic potentialities of a person are empowerment and excellence. Empowerment refers to the strength or power to accomplish goals, and excellence signifies the quality to do one's best.

Empowerers, motivated by caring and achieving, find fulfillment in helping and seeing individuals develop their unique talents. Caring Empowerers encourage, support, instruct, and share power with others. They help others appreciate the value of their work and life, personal power, and aspirations.

Strong in critical times, Empowerers challenge others to be steadfast and remain faithful to their values. Empowerers call others to be aware of their strengths and potentialities for development as they encounter challenging situations.

Excellors have the capacity to be their best. Motivated by caring and achieving, they enable others to excel in their work. They are aware of their own significance and the things that contribute to their self-worth. They are ready and willing to acknowledge to themselves and others when they feel good and when they are not satisfied with themselves or situations.

Although Excellors aim for perfection, their positive perspective enables them to accept the limitations of human existence. Their ideal is to be the best they can be as they strive for growth as people. Animated by caring and achieving, Excellors focus on the talents and gifts of persons and help bring them to perfection.

## Activators

The five activators of a person's nature are Knower, Feeler, Belonger, Harmonizer, and Achiever. These activators effect mental action (Knower, Feeler), relational action (Belonger, Harmonizer), and behavioral action (Achiever).

*Knowers.* Knowers activate perceptions, images, ideas, and theories in order to observe and understand people and things. They realize that, as they strive to solve problems, some questions may be unanswered. At ease with not comprehending everything, Knowers are comfortable acknowledging that sometimes they may not be able to explain confusing situations. They like to respond to the challenge of puzzling problems by wondering and questioning, by exploring and discovering ways of figuring out what is happening. After making sense of what is going on in life and their work, Knowers can clearly articulate the significance of personal and interpersonal experiences. Motivated by caring and achieving, they help others understand the meaning of their personal and professional experiences and formulate goals. The Knower is complemented by the Feeler.

*Feelers.* Knowing flows from the cognitive side of a person's nature, whereas feeling springs from its affective side. In touch with their own feelings, Feelers are comfortable sharing them with other people. Motivated by self-caring, they accept their positive feelings and themselves. The empathy of Feelers enables them to appreciate how others experience themselves in the world; they intuit what others are feeling. Feelers sense whether other people feel pleased or uncomfortable. Animated by caring, Feelers help others feel in touch with their feelings and express them in appropriate ways. Feelers also sense what is personally significant to people. The caring Feeler supports others by actively listening not only to the speaker's words but also to his or her feelings. As a result, others tend to feel accepted and understood.

*Belongers.* Belongers are oriented toward relationships; they bond with others and find fulfillment by connecting in positive ways. They respect the value of people and are faithful to their interpersonal commitments. Motivated by caring, they can form lasting and nurturing relationships with others. Belongers are loyal to their friends and the organizations and communities to which they are committed. They tend to identify with the traditions and customs of an organization and claim its objectives and tasks as their own. They can be trusted to do their work and fulfill their responsibilities.

*Harmonizers.* Harmonizers supplement Belongers by maintaining or restoring peace within an organization or community. Stable and serene, Harmonizers accept different people, help people feel at ease, and facilitate their getting along. With a gift for mediation, they can balance opposing views in their mind as they work for agreement.

*Achiever.* Achievers project goals and coordinate ways to attain them. Driven by the desire to achieve, Achievers are single-minded and assertive in pursuit of their goals. Motivated by caring, they help others stay on track toward their goals. After putting first things first, they concentrate their energies and efforts on what is useful to get results. Unswerving in centering on their goals, they are steadfast and resolute in their determination to succeed. Achievers progress toward their goals by directing their resources efficiently. They plan activities, organize tasks, conduct meetings, and foster team effectiveness. Achievers are adaptable to changing situations and new ideas from other people while being structured in organizing projects.

## Integration of Self

Even though the motivators, potentiators, and activators perform different functions, they are rooted in a person's nature. These three forces complement one another:

- The three motivators are why a person acts—out of Caring, Achieving, and Fulfilling; they are the reasons a person acts.

- The two potentiators are who or what operates—the Empowerer and Excellor; they are the agency that functions.

■ The five activators are the ways a person energizes—Knowing, Feeling, Belonging, Harmonizing, and Achieving; they are how to get into action.

A physiological model for understanding these concepts is the left and right hemisphere of the brain. The left hemisphere, which controls the right side of the body, enjoys linguistic, mechanical, rational, deductive, analytic, and motor functions. Right hemisphere functions are spatial, holistic, artistic, emotional, intuitive, imaginative, and contemplative.

The Excellor, Achiever, Knower, and Empowerer functions reside in the left brain. The Carer, Feeler, Belonger, and Fulfiller functions reside in the right brain. The Harmonizer, like the brain's corpus callosum, connects the right and left functions.

Another model for understanding these concepts is psychological: Carl Jung's animus and anima. On the one hand, animus refers to the inner male orientation toward reason, meaning, power, strength, knowledge, values, and goals. On the other hand, anima signifies the inner female orientation toward feeling, life, creativity, relationships, and love. A unified self is a unity of animus and anima, a unity of opposites.

The fully functioning human being moves toward peak self-empowerment by doing what it takes to be more and more integrated within and without the self. Integration of the total person and all that is good in this life an essential goal for every person.

*"There is not accident in our choice of reading.*
*All our sources are related."*

— François Mauriac

# 16

# SELECTED BIBLIOGRAPHY

Aspell, D.D., & Aspell, P.J. (1990). *Chart of the Enneagram Personality Types.* San Antonio, TX: Lifewings® Ltd.

Aspell, D.D., & Aspell, P.J. (1991). *The Enneagram Inventory®: Revised and Extended Version. Third Edition.* San Antonio, TX: Lifewings® Ltd.

Aspell, D.D., & Aspell, P.J. (1991). *Profiles of the Enneagram: Ways of Coming Home to Yourself.* San Antonio, TX: Lifewings® Ltd.

Aspell, D.D., & Aspell, P.J. (1992). *Unlimited Empowerment: Discovering and Enhancing Your Personal Professional Life via the Enneagram.* San Antonio, TX: Lifewings® Ltd.

Aspell, D.D., & Aspell, P.J. (1993). *Empowering Relationships: Discovering and Enhancing Your Personal and Interpersonal Life via the Enneagram.* San Antonio, TX: Lifewings® Ltd.

Aspell, D.D., & Aspell, P.J. (1994). *The Archetype Inventory.* San Antonio, TX: Lifewings® Ltd.

Aspell, D.D., & Aspell, P.J. (1994). *Profiles of the Nine Personal Professional Enneagram Styles.* San Antonio, TX: Lifewings® Ltd.

Aspell, D.D., & Aspell, P.J. (1995). *Building Better Relationships with People.* San Antonio, TX: Lifewings® Ltd.

Aspell, D.D., & Aspell, P.J. (1995). *Career and Life Management.* San Antonio, TX: Lifewings® Ltd.

Aspell, D.D., & Aspell, P.J. (1995). *Chart of the Nine Enneagram Personality Types and Professional Styles.* San Antonio, TX: Lifewings® Ltd.

Aspell, D.D., & Aspell, P.J. (1995). *Creating Teams and Building Teamwork.* San Antonio, TX: Lifewings® Ltd.

Aspell, D.D., & Aspell, P.J. (1995). *The Discovery and Development of Effective Personal Leadership.* San Antonio, TX: Lifewings® Ltd.

Aspell, D.D., & Aspell, P.J. (1995). *Discovering Yourself and Developing Your Style of Leadership, Supervision, and Counseling.* San Antonio, TX: Lifewings® Ltd.

Aspell, D.D., & Aspell, P.J. (1995). *Enneagram Communication Styles.* San Antonio, TX: Lifewings® Ltd.

Aspell, D.D., & Aspell, P.J. (1995). *The Enneagram Inventory®: Abbreviated Version.* San Antonio, TX: Lifewings® Ltd.

Aspell, D.D., & Aspell, P.J. (1995). *The Enneagram Inventory® for Deacons.* San Antonio, TX: Lifewings® Ltd.

Aspell, D.D., & Aspell, P.J. (1995). *Enneagram Learning Styles.* San Antonio, TX: Lifewings® Ltd.

Aspell, D.D., & Aspell, P.J. (1995). *Enneagram Teaching and Training Styles.* San Antonio, TX: Lifewings® Ltd.

Aspell, D.D., & Aspell, P.J. (1995). *Enneagram Thinking and Problem-Solving Styles.* San Antonio, TX: Lifewings® Ltd.

Aspell, D.D., & Aspell, P.J. (1995). *Enneagram Transparencies.* San Antonio, TX: Lifewings® Ltd.

Aspell, D.D., & Aspell, P.J. (1995). *Enneagram Transparencies for Christian Applications.* San Antonio, TX: Lifewings® Ltd.

Aspell, D.D., & Aspell, P.J. (1995). *How to Use the Enneagram for Effective Counseling.* San Antonio, TX: Lifewings® Ltd.

Aspell, D.D., & Aspell, P.J. (1995). Leadership Styles and the Enneagram, in J.W. Pfeiffer (Ed.), *The 1995 Annual: Volume 1, Training* (pp. 227-241). San Francisco: Pfeiffer, An Imprint of Jossey-Bass Inc., Publishers.

Aspell, D.D., & Aspell, P.J. (1995). *Letting Go of Irritants.* San Antonio, TX: Lifewings® Ltd.

Aspell, D.D., & Aspell, P.J. (1995). *Managing Conflict the Enneagram Way.* San Antonio, TX: Lifewings® Ltd.

Aspell, D.D., & Aspell, P.J. (1995). *Using the Enneagram to Build Better Marital Relationships.* San Antonio, TX: Lifewings® Ltd.

Aspell, D.D., & Aspell, P.J. (1995). *Using the Enneagram to Empower Organizations.* San Antonio, TX: Lifewings® Ltd.

Aspell, D.D., & Aspell, P.J. (1996). *The Eloquent Enneagrammer: Quality Presentation and Speaking.* San Antonio, TX: Lifewings® Ltd.

Aspell, D.D., & Aspell, P.J. (1996). *The Enneagram Inventory® and The Jungian Personality Type Inventory™.* San Antonio, TX: Lifewings® Ltd.

Aspell, D.D., & Aspell, P.J. (1996). *Enneagram Portraits of Ministers.* San Antonio, TX: Lifewings® Ltd.

Aspell, D.D., & Aspell, P.J. (1996). *Enneagram Portraits of Pastoral Administrators.* San Antonio, TX: Lifewings® Ltd.

Aspell, D.D., & Aspell, P.J. (1996). *Enneagram Portraits of Priests.* San Antonio, TX: Lifewings® Ltd.

Aspell, D.D., & Aspell, P.J. (1996). *The Enterprising Enneagrammer: How to Use the Enneagram to Make Sales.* San Antonio, TX: Lifewings® Ltd.

Aspell, D.D., & Aspell, P.J. (1996). *Journey from Type to Archetype: Jungian Personality Type Inventory™ and Archetype Inventory™.* San Antonio, TX: Lifewings® Ltd.

Aspell, D.D., & Aspell, P.J. (1996). *The Jungian Personality Type Inventory™.* San Antonio, TX: Lifewings® Ltd.

Aspell, D.D., & Aspell, P.J. (1996). *The Enneagram for Lawyers.* San Antonio, TX: Lifewings® Ltd.

Aspell, D.D., & Aspell, P.J. (1996). *Managing Diversity.* San Antonio, TX: Lifewings® Ltd.

Aspell, D.D., & Aspell, P.J. (1996). *The Nine Enneagram Negotiation Styles.* San Antonio, TX: Lifewings® Ltd.

Aspell, D.D., & Aspell, P.J. (1996). *Portraits of Enneagram Relationships: Nine Relational and Forty-Five Interpersonal Enneagram Relationships.* San Antonio, TX: Lifewings® Ltd.

Aspell, D.D., & Aspell, P.J. (1996). *Using the Enneagram to Build Better Christian Marriages.* San Antonio, TX: Lifewings® Ltd.

Covey, S.R. (1990). *The Seven Habits of Highly Effective People.* New York: Simon & Schuster.

Covey, S.R. (1991). *Principle-Centered Leadership.* New York: Simon & Schuster.

Forster, S., & O'Hanrahan, R. (1994). *Understanding Personality Types in the Workplace.* Oakland, CA: Authors.

Palmer, H. (1995). *The Enneagram in Love and Work.* San Francisco: HarperCollins.

*Note:* The Enneagram Inventory® has been tested for reliability. For the results, see G. C. Leeper, *A Study of the Reliability of the Aspell Enneagram Inventory®,* Research Project Report, 1996, The University of Texas of The Permian Basin. Further research is in progress in the Graduate School of Education.

*"The motto should not be: Forgive one another;
rather, Understand one another."*

— Emma Goldman

# APPENDIX A:
# SUMMARY CHARTS OF KEY TRAITS

| Key Traits of ONES | |
|---|---|
| TALENTS | To seek excellence and correctness; at best, to journey toward optimism. |
| THINKING PATTERNS | To be the Idealist, guided by high standards and moral thinking; to reason on the basis of principles. |
| COMMUNICATION STYLE | To communicate about what is right and correct; to speak authoritatively; to be straightforward and direct; to sermonize or instruct. |
| COPING STYLE | To repress or displace anger. |
| INTEGRAL FEELINGS | To be angry at imperfections; zealous for good; serene. |
| CORE MOTIVATION | To be right; to be not criticized. |
| APPROACH TO WORK | To act in correct, methodical ways, with clear roles; to prefer competent and fair leaders; to like organized work. |
| APPROACH TO RELATIONSHIPS | To associate love with good behavior; to control others by rules; to express caring in conventional ways. |
| CHALLENGES | To avoid falling into being judgmental, intolerant, rigid, or perfectionist. |
| DIRECTION OF GROWTH | To relax; to pay attention to the positive; to practice patience and humor; to channel anger constructively. |

| Key Traits of TWOS | |
|---|---|
| TALENTS | To seek to love, care for, and help others; at best, to journey toward awareness of own needs. |
| THINKING PATTERNS | To be Affective; to think of others' needs; to reason from the heart and feelings; to be person oriented. |
| COMMUNICATION STYLE | To communicate about ways of being helpful; to express warmth and friendliness; to listen with empathy; to like one-on-one conversations; to flatter. |
| COPING STYLE | To identify with others' needs; to repress own needs; to deny negative feelings. |
| INTEGRAL FEELINGS | To be afraid of being rejected or not needed; to feel love and warmth in being accepted. |
| CORE MOTIVATION | To love and help; to be appreciated. |
| APPROACH TO WORK | To help authority to win support; to be effective socially; to like coworkers with similar attitudes; to like helping the needy. |
| APPROACH TO RELATIONSHIPS | To please others to win affection; to rely on others' approval; to support others' goals; to tend to control others. |
| CHALLENGES | To avoid falling into being pushy, overly solicitous, or possessive of others. |
| DIRECTION OF GROWTH | To care for others' real needs; to allow good works to speak for themselves; to share friendships with others. |

| Key Traits of THREES | |
|---|---|
| TALENTS | To seek to succeed; to set goals and organize; to be excellent communicators and motivators; at best, to find an identity as part of a group. |
| THINKING PATTERNS | To be Practical; to consider the results to be achieved; to calculate useful means to reach objectives; to see ideas as tools for getting things done. |
| COMMUNICATION STYLE | To communicate by talking persuasively; to project a winning image; to advertise and propagandize; to speak energetically. |
| COPING STYLE | To repress fearful feelings of rejection; to project blame on others; to identify with achievement. |
| INTEGRAL FEELINGS | To be afraid of being rejected or being a failure; to be desirable and worthwhile. |
| CORE MOTIVATION | To be affirmed by others; to create an attractive image of themselves. |
| APPROACH TO WORK | To prefer leadership to achieve success; to be competitive; to like jobs with status; to motivate others to act; to tend toward workaholism. |
| APPROACH TO RELATIONSHIPS | To relate in terms of a role to be performed; to like the accomplishments of friends; to view intimacy as doing rather than being; to enjoy social activities. |
| CHALLENGES | To avoid falling into being unaware of feelings, obsessed with social status, or opportunistic. |
| DIRECTION OF GROWTH | To cooperate; to have genuine concern for others' feelings and needs; to affirm and respect others; to practice self-acceptance. |

| Key Traits of FOURS | |
|---|---|
| TALENTS | To seek deeper awareness of feelings; at best, to journey toward self-renewal and self-acceptance. |
| THINKING PATTERNS | To be the Personalist; to judge according to what is important personally; to reason from feelings; to allow moods to color perceptions of facts and truth. |
| COMMUNICATION STYLE | To communicate with sensitivity; to speak with feeling; to allow moods to influence tone of voice; to use dramatic expressions; to be a sympathetic listener. |
| COPING STYLE | To internalize unacceptable feelings; to displace or sublimate feelings into symbols and art. |
| INTEGRAL FEELINGS | To be afraid of being inadequate or lacking; to have emotional ups and downs. |
| CORE MOTIVATION | To understand who they are; to contact their feelings. |
| APPROACH TO WORK | To see possibilities in ordinary situations; to lead in a distinctive way; to like jobs where their special talents are recognized. |
| APPROACH TO RELATIONSHIPS | To perceive others' negative features when close and their positive traits when distant; to help others through crises; to share feelings. |
| CHALLENGES | To avoid falling into being self-absorbed, hypersensitive, or moody. |
| DIRECTION OF GROWTH | To manage feelings; to allow the head to rule over the heart; to focus on positive experiences; to choose a consistent, self-disciplined way of living. |

| Key Traits of FIVES | |
|---|---|
| TALENTS | To seek to observe, understand, and explain; at best, to journey toward confidence and assertiveness. |
| THINKING PATTERNS | To be the Analytical; to analyze problems, observe facts, and reason logically; to reason from evidence; to connect ideas into a meaningful whole. |
| COMMUNICATION STYLE | To communicate through ideas and theories; to summarize in a coherent manner; to economize with words, focusing on essential ideas; to generalize in abstract statements. |
| COPING STYLE | To isolate thoughts from unpleasant feelings; to project theories on facts. |
| INTEGRAL FEELINGS | To be afraid of unfamiliar social situations and of unpredictable emotions; to be alert, curious, and confident. |
| CORE MOTIVATION | To know everything with certainty, to avoid ignorance. |
| APPROACH TO WORK | To prefer to work for themselves, with minimal supervision; to want to be clearly informed; to be able to plan long-range projects. |
| APPROACH TO RELATIONSHIPS | To shift between intimacy and distance; to withdraw from others' intense emotions; to be defensive when their ideas are criticized. |
| CHALLENGES | To avoid falling away from contact with feelings and withdrawing in social interactions. |
| DIRECTION OF GROWTH | To face reality; to relax the mind; to be aware of feelings; to learn caring and assertiveness. |

## Key Traits of SIXES

| | |
|---|---|
| TALENTS | To seek to relate to others; to be loyal; to respect authority and traditions; at best, to journey toward stable emotions. |
| THINKING PATTERNS | To be Authoritative; to base thinking on the authority of the leader, tradition, or rules; to identify with group thinking. |
| COMMUNICATION STYLE | To communicate established opinions and views; to be careful in speech; to promote warm and friendly communication within the group; to be cautious outside the group. |
| COPING STYLE | To identify with an authority figure; to displace anger on people outside of the group; to project suspicions on outsiders. |
| INTEGRAL FEELINGS | To be afraid of being abandoned or alone; to be insecure; to be self-affirmed and courageous. |
| CORE MOTIVATION | To be safe and secure; to belong to a group for approval. |
| APPROACH TO WORK | To feel safe in a like-minded group; to identify with victims; to prefer a clear chain of command; to delay tough decisions; to like jobs with clear roles and goals. |
| APPROACH TO RELATIONSHIPS | To be slow to trust and commit themselves; to be giving and supportive once they are secure; to be afraid of being taken advantage of by a powerful person. |
| CHALLENGES | To avoid losing faith in self; to avoid over reliance on authority; to avoid insecurity. |
| DIRECTION OF GROWTH | To manage fear and anger; to trust in the ability to relate to people; to affirm self with positive thinking. |

| Key Traits of SEVENS | |
|---|---|
| TALENTS | To seek to enjoy life; to do many things well; to see creative possibilities; at best, to journey toward deeper insights. |
| THINKING PATTERNS | To be Positive; to focus on possibilities; to consider new and different approaches; to plan for future enjoyment. |
| COMMUNICATION STYLE | To communicate about what is pleasant and enjoyable; to like telling stories, using lively metaphors and a light, humorous style; to ask different questions; to gossip. |
| COPING STYLE | To repress anxiety; to flee from an inner life; to act out impulses; to sublimate unpleasant experiences into an apparent good. |
| INTEGRAL FEELINGS | To be afraid of discomfort and pain; to be thankful and joyful. |
| CORE MOTIVATION | To be happy; to avoid pain and anxiety. |
| APPROACH TO WORK | To want authority to respect their freedoms; to promote a positive mood in a group; to see exciting visions of new ideas and projects; to be bored by routine. |
| APPROACH TO RELATIONSHIPS | To enjoy sharing positive experiences with others; to have difficulty being tied down by commitment; to maximize time doing interesting things. |
| CHALLENGES | To avoid falling into craving for amusement and fun and indulging appetites impulsively. |
| DIRECTION OF GROWTH | To moderate impulses; to be happier with less; to discover what is best; to experience the truly satisfying. |

| Key Traits of EIGHTS | |
|---|---|
| TALENTS | To seek to be confident and assertive as natural leaders; at best, to journey toward helping others. |
| THINKING PATTERNS | To be Dialectical; to dictate opposing opinions; to believe that knowledge is power; to express ideas forcefully. |
| COMMUNICATION STYLE | To communicate about what is fair and just; to be blunt and direct; to speak forcefully and with confidence; to use commands and exclamations. |
| COPING STYLE | To deny weakness; to repress gentle feelings; to react aggressively. |
| INTEGRAL FEELINGS | To be aggressive and angry; to be confident, forebearing, and benevolent. |
| CORE MOTIVATION | To be self-reliant; to avoid submitting to others; to be driven by the will to power. |
| APPROACH TO WORK | To serve as born leaders, motivating others to achieve goals; to protect others from unfair treatment; to function best when in charge of tasks completely. |
| APPROACH TO RELATIONSHIPS | To base relationships on agreements and doing things with passion; to be slow to disclose feelings and be vulnerable; to dominate others. |
| CHALLENGES | To avoid falling into being tough and dominating others for own self-interest. |
| DIRECTION OF GROWTH | To balance justice and compassion; to enjoy the power of serving others; to use leadership for great deeds and opportunities for others. |

| Key Traits of NINES | |
|---|---|
| TALENTS | To seek to be accepting, easy going, stable, and trusting; at best, to journey toward energy and enthusiasm. |
| THINKING PATTERNS | To be Holistic; to unify parts into a harmonious whole; to play down differences; to grasp similarities; to emphasize what is agreeable. |
| COMMUNICATION STYLE | To communicate about what is agreeable; to avoid what is provocative; to speak in a relaxed, calm manner; to use matter-of-fact, monotone speech; to listen patiently. |
| COPING STYLE | To repress conflicting feelings and anger; to dissociate thoughts from aggressive impulses; to deny the existence of problems. |
| INTEGRAL FEELINGS | To be relaxed and at peace; to be afraid of separation from others through conflict; to be patient, energetic, and self-possessed. |
| CORE MOTIVATION | To live in unity and harmony with others; to maintain peace. |
| APPROACH TO WORK | To be good leaders when clear about purpose; to be excellent mediators; to tend to gloss over problems; to prefer clear guidelines from authority. |
| APPROACH TO RELATIONSHIPS | To make others' interests their own; to believe that love means merging with the other person's thinking and feelings; to accept without judging others. |
| CHALLENGES | To avoid falling into being too accommodating or withdrawing from disagreements. |
| DIRECTION OF GROWTH | To respond to challenges; to deal directly with disagreements; to develop the inner strength to handle crises. |

*"The world is quite right. It does not have to be consistent."*

— Charlotte Perkins Gilman

# APPENDIX B:
# SUMMARY CHARTS OF CONGRUENCE

| Matching Behaviors and Words for ONES | |
|---|---|
| EYE CONTACT | Direct and steady. |
| HANDSHAKE | Firm. |
| GESTURES | Controlled and limited. |
| PROXIMITY | Near or far. |
| COMMUNICATION PATTERN | Speaking carefully; stating accurate facts; using an even inflection in voice; maintaining moderate volume and constant tempo. |
| SELF-IMAGE | Neat; well groomed; formal; erect posture. |
| SELF-TALK | "I am correct and right." |
| PERSONAL NOTES | |

| Matching Behaviors and Words for TWOS | |
|---|---|
| EYE CONTACT | Direct and steady. |
| HANDSHAKE | Gentle. |
| GESTURES | Spontaneous; touching others. |
| PROXIMITY | Near. |
| COMMUNICATION PATTERN | Speaking warmly; using variety in inflection; using low volume and a somewhat quick tempo. |
| SELF-IMAGE | Friendly; smiling; kind; lending a helping hand. |
| SELF-TALK | "I am helpful and caring." |
| PERSONAL NOTES | |

| Matching Behaviors and Words for THREES | |
|---|---|
| EYE CONTACT | Direct and continual. |
| HANDSHAKE | Firm. |
| GESTURES | Spontaneous. |
| PROXIMITY | Near. |
| COMMUNICATION PATTERN | Speaking efficiently and persuasively; using variety in inflection; using loud volume and quick tempo. |
| SELF-IMAGE | Doing things and getting results; active. |
| SELF-TALK | "I am likeable and successful." |
| PERSONAL NOTES | |

| Matching Behaviors and Words for FOURS | |
|---|---|
| EYE CONTACT | Intermittent and gentle. |
| HANDSHAKE | Firm or light. |
| GESTURES | Spontaneous. |
| PROXIMITY | Near or far. |
| COMMUNICATION PATTERN | Listening with sympathy; talking according to mood; using much or little inflection; using high or low volume and fast or slow tempo. |
| SELF-IMAGE | Expressive of feelings; unique appearance and clothing. |
| SELF-TALK | "I am sensitive and unique." |
| PERSONAL NOTES | |

| Matching Behaviors and Words for FIVES | |
|---|---|
| EYE CONTACT | Intermittent. |
| HANDSHAKE | Light. |
| GESTURES | Limited and controlled. |
| PROXIMITY | Distant. |
| COMMUNICATION PATTERN | Listening reflectively; keeping opinions to self; using even inflection, low volume, and slow tempo. |
| SELF-IMAGE | Hand on chin or cheek; wrapped up in thought; quizzical looks. |
| SELF-TALK | "I am intelligent and knowledgeable." |
| PERSONAL NOTES | |

| Matching Behaviors and Words for SIXES | |
|---|---|
| EYE CONTACT | Intermittent. |
| HANDSHAKE | Gentle. |
| GESTURES | Controlled; hands on chest (loyalty). |
| PROXIMITY | Near people in own group. |
| COMMUNICATION PATTERN | Listening attentively; speaking whatever is agreeable to the group; using even inflection, moderate volume, and steady tempo. |
| SELF-IMAGE | Hard working; cooperative. |
| SELF-TALK | "I am reliable and loyal." |
| PERSONAL NOTES | |

THE ENNEAGRAM PERSONALITY PORTRAITS

| Matching Behaviors and Words for SEVENS | |
|---|---|
| EYE CONTACT | Direct and steady. |
| HANDSHAKE | Firm. |
| GESTURES | Spontaneous. |
| PROXIMITY | Near. |
| COMMUNICATION PATTERN | Speaking positively and optimistically; using variety in inflection; using loud volume and steady tempo. |
| SELF-IMAGE | Active in doing things; smiling and cheerful. |
| SELF-TALK | "I am happy and enjoying myself." |
| PERSONAL NOTES | |

| Matching Behaviors and Words for EIGHTS | |
|---|---|
| EYE CONTACT | Firm and strong. |
| HANDSHAKE | Firm and strong. |
| GESTURES | Spontaneous; hands on hips. |
| PROXIMITY | Distant. |
| COMMUNICATION PATTERN | Speaking forcefully; using a commanding voice; using variety in inflection, loud volume, and fast tempo. |
| SELF-IMAGE | Jutting jaw; firm mouth; eyes set; erect posture. |
| SELF-TALK | "I am confident and assertive." |
| PERSONAL NOTES | |

| Matching Behaviors and Words for NINES | |
|---|---|
| EYE CONTACT | Intermittent. |
| HANDSHAKE | Gentle. |
| GESTURES | Controlled; welcoming with open hands. |
| PROXIMITY | Near. |
| COMMUNICATION PATTERN | Listening receptively; saying what is agreeable; using even inflection, low volume, and slow tempo. |
| SELF-IMAGE | Relaxed; easy going. |
| SELF-TALK | "I am peaceful and calm." |
| PERSONAL NOTES | |

*"In a world where there is so much to be done, I felt strongly impressed that there must be something for me to do."*

— Dorothea Dix

# ABOUT THE AUTHORS

The co-authors are a unique team that blends theory and practice. In the words of the Enneagram, Patrick is the Observer who gathers data, reflects on ideas, and explains things, while Dee Dee is the Achiever who acts on the ideas, publishes, and communicates them.

Patrick is the Thinker who analyzes and theorizes about a project, while Dee Dee is a Producer who works to get results and complete tasks. Patrick is a Systematizer who organizes concepts into a grand vision, while Dee Dee is a Motivator who activates people and resources to attain their goals.

Aware of the unlimited possibilities of life, they believe that their mission is to be the best as they share their talents with others. They find fulfillment in caring and helping others grow in their gifts. They enjoy participating in the human project and empowering their fellow human beings with a feel for excellence, insight, empathy, a sense of team and cooperation, and the joy of being productive.

They are a professional husband-wife team who are consultants in private practice in San Antonio, Texas. Dee Dee earned her M.A. in Clinical Psychology from St. Mary's University. Patrick earned his Ph.D. in Psychology from United States International University and his Ph.D. in Philosophy and S.T.L. in Theology from Catholic University of America.

Their training at Wilford Hall Medical Center and Raleigh Hills Hospital, their participation in advanced personal and professional workshops, and their combined 45 years of counseling experience enable them to function with professional insights and skills.

Their seminars, workshops, and presentations for departments of defense personnel, educational and religious groups, and professional counselors have been well received and effective in empowering people's personal and professional lives. Their eclectic and challenging approach draws on their insights and proficiency in psychology, philosophy, and theology, with advanced workshops in personal and professional development.

As a public service to the community, they have appeared on television to discuss topics such as mid-life transitions, communication, conflict management, and personality development. Their volunteer work as counselors and advisors to the Texas Teenage Crime Commission contributes to helping troubled teenagers. Dee Dee enjoys being a mentor at Business Careers High School.

One of their deepest fulfillments is in caring for and helping their son Patrick, Jr., enjoy excelling in his life and work. Their family never ceases to wonder at the loyalty and friendliness of Liz—their dog!

## Contact Information

The Aspells encourage readers to contact them with questions or observations:

Lifewings®, Ltd.
P.O. Box 460688
San Antonio, Texas 78246-0688
Phone: 210-829-7107
FAX: 210-828-0965
e-mail: aspell@txdirect.com

# INDEX

## A

Accepters, 65-69
  color symbolism for, 105
Accommodating relationships, 96-97
Achievers, 15, 29, 31, 116
  color symbolism for, 102
Activators, 115-116
Affective thinking style, 24
Aggressiveness, 14, 95
Analytical thinking, 42.
  *See also* Thinking style
Animators, 53-54, 68
Animus/anima model, 117
Anxiety, avoidance of, 55
Appeasers, 32
Appreciation
  in ONES, 19
  in TWOS, 25
  in THREES, 31
  in FOURS, 37
  in FIVES, 43
  in SIXES, 49
  in SEVENS, 55
  in EIGHTS, 61-62
  in NINES, 67
Approach-withdrawal relationships,
  81-82
Approval, in SIXES, 49
Arrows of development, 8, 9-12
Aspell, Dee Dee, 143-144
Aspell, Patrick, 143-144
Asserters, 59-60
Assertiveness, 14, 59, 93, 94
Authority, ambivalence about, 50
Awareness, personal, 96

## B

Balance
  in TWOS, 27
  in FOURS, 39
  in FIVES, 45
  in SIXES, 51
  in EIGHTS, 63, 95
Behavior
  character and, 2,
  controlling, 72
Beliefs
  of ONES, 19
  of TWOS, 24-25
  of THREES, 30-31
  of FOURS, 37
  of FIVES, 42-43
  of SIXES, 49
  of SEVENS, 55
  of EIGHTS, 61
  of NINES, 66-67

Belongers, 115-116
Blue, symbolism of, 105
Bossiness, 10
Brain hemispheres, 117
Brown, symbolism of, 103
Browning, Robert, 6
Bullies, 26
Business, Enneagram training
  applications for, 108-111.
  *See also* Organizations

## C

Carers, 23
  color symbolism for, 101-102
Caring, 12, 13
  as a motivation, 25
Challengers, 15, 59-63
  color symbolism for, 104
Challenging relationships, 93-95
Charts of congruence, 133-141
Cheerers, 53-57
  color symbolism for, 104
Collaboration, 48, 66, 91
  among team members, 110-111
Colors, Enneagram types and, 101-105
Commitment, 10, 13
  questioning of, 96
  to relationships, 75
Communication
  clear, 86
  expressiveness in, 35
  in ONES, 73
  in TWOS, 76
  in THREES, 78-79
  in FOURS, 81-82
  in FIVES, 84-85
  in SIXES, 48, 88
  in SEVENS, 91
  in EIGHTS, 94
  in NINES, 97
Compassion, 10, 13
Competition, 60
  THREES and, 79
Conciliation, working toward, 88
Conflict, retreat from, 68
Conflict management
  by ONES, 73
  by TWOS, 76
  by THREES, 79
  by FOURS, 82
  by FIVES, 85
  by SIXES, 88
  by SEVENS, 91
  by EIGHTS, 94
  by NINES, 98
Conformity, to group thinking, 48

Confrontation
  discomfort with, 66
  dislike of, 54
Confucius, 46
Control issues, 19, 93
Corporations, Enneagram theory and, 3
Cosmic connectedness, 86
Cosmic laws, 80, 89-90
  participation in, 96
Cosmic process, 77
Cosmic spirit, 99
Cosmos, wonder of, 92
Creativity, 10, 13
Creators, 35
  color symbolism for, 102-103

**D**

Deception, 11
Decision making.
  *See also* Problem solving
  rational, 42
  in TWOS, 75
  in SIXES, 48
  in EIGHTS, 61
Decline
  arrows of, 7-15
  direction of, 8-9
Denial, of problems, 98
de Sales, Frances, 58
Detail, attention to, 18
Development
  arrows and wings of, 7-15
  direction of, 9
Dialectical thinking, 60
Dictators, 26, 62
Differences, matching, 109
Directors, 44, 60, 62
Disagreements, resolving, 76
Disconnectedness, 11
Discord, avoidance of, 67
Dix, Dorothea, 142
Dogmatism, 20
Duty, attention to, 13, 14

**E**

Economy, law of, 92
Effectiveness, interpersonal, 72
Ego, personal, 3
EIGHTS, 15, 59-63
  arrows of development for, 11-12
  chart of congruence for, 140
  key traits of, 130
  relational style of, 93-95
  wings of development for, 14
Eliot, George, 28
Emerson, Ralph Waldo, 52
Emotional distance, 93

Emotional honesty, 37
Emotional issues, 72
  *See also* Feelings
Emotionality, 10
Emotional withdrawal, 84
Empathy, 11
Empowerers, 114
Empowerment, 2, 4, 20, 113, 114
  of personalities, 72
  of professional style, 37
  of ONES, 21
  of TWOS, 27
  of THREES, 33
  of FOURS, 39
  of FIVES, 44, 45
  of SIXES, 51
  of SEVENS, 56, 57
  of EIGHTS, 63
  of NINES, 69
Enneagram
  applications of, 107-111
  benefits of, 4-5
  business applications of, 108-111
  in the corporate world, 2-3
  defined, 1-2
  insights offered by, 4-5
  meaning of, 2-4
  origins of, 1-5
  relationship insights of, 71-72
Enneagram Inventory and Profile®, 107
Enneagram types.
  *See also* Personality
  colors and, 101-105
  influences on, 8-9
  studying, 107
  understanding, 7
Entrepreneurship, 61
Environment, harmony with, 83
Excellors, 114
Exhibitionists, 56
Exploiters, 50
Expressionists, 25, 35-36
Extroversion, 14

**F**

Failure, avoidance of, 79
Fairness, 18
Fear, 11
Feelers, 115
Feelings.
  *See also* Emotional issues
  disconnecting from, 44
  fear of, 93
  insecure, 50
  making conclusions based on, 36
First International Enneagram Conference, 3
FIVES, 41-45
  arrows of development for, 11

chart of congruence for, 137
key traits of, 127
relational style of, 83-86
wings of development for, 13-14
FOURS, 35-39
    arrows of development for, 10
    chart of congruence for, 136
    key traits of, 126
    relational style of, 80-83
    wings of development for, 13
Friendliness, 13, 90, 101
Friendship, 97

**G**

Generosity, 25
Gilman, Charlotte Perkins, 132
Givingness, 87
Goethe, Johann Wolfgang von, 40
Golden Rule, 71, 108
Goldman, Emma, 122
Gray, symbolism of, 103
Green, symbolism of, 102
Gregariousness, 13
Groupists, 47
    color symbolism for, 103
Group mindedness, 13, 48, 88
Growth, choosing, 15
Growth avenues
    for ONES, 74-75
    for TWOS, 77
    for THREES, 80
    for FOURS, 83
    for FIVES, 86
    for SIXES, 89-90
    for SEVENS, 92-93
    for EIGHTS, 95-96
    for NINES, 99
Gurdjieff, George I., 2

**H**

Harmonizers, 116
Helpers, 23, 25, 62
Helping relationships, 75-76
Hierarchical organizations, 89
Hinkle, Beatrice, 34
Holistic thinking, 66
Humanistic organizational climate, 36

**I**

Ichazo, Oscar, 2
Idealism, 13
Idealists, 18-19
Image, attractive, 31
Image projection, 78-79
Imbalance, talent development and, 14-15.
    *See also* Balance
Impulsivity, 11, 56
Indecision, 12
Individual differences, 71

Individualist, 36
Individuality, preserving, 96
Individuals, focus on, 36
Inferiority, feelings of, 50
Inflexibility, 74
Inner authority, 90
Innovation, 14, 55, 91
Insecurity, 50, 103
Insight, 11
    appreciation for, 43
Instability, 11
Integrity
    compromising, 30
    regard for, 19
Intellectualizing, 44
Intellectual pursuits, devotion to, 84
Intellectual relationships, 83-84
Interpersonal style, developing, 108-109
Intimacy, 78, 90
Intolerance, 11, 74
Introspection, 35, 103
Introversion, 14, 80, 87
Irritants
    for ONES, 74
    for TWOS, 77
    for THREES, 79-80
    for FOURS, 82-83
    for FIVES, 86
    for SIXES, 89
    for SEVENS, 92
    for EIGHTS, 95
    for NINES, 98

**J**

Jealousy, 10
Joyfulness, 14
Judgmentalism, 13, 20
Jung, Carl, 7, 117

**K**

Key traits, chart of, 123-131
Knowers, 115

**L**

Laziness, 10
Leadership, 11
    strong, 61
Leadership style
    empowerment of, 25
    of ONES, 18
    of TWOS, 24
    of THREES, 30
    of FOURS, 36
    of FIVES, 42, 44
    of SIXES, 48, 50
    of SEVENS, 54
    of EIGHTS, 60
    of NINES, 66

Left hemisphere functions, 117
LeGuin, Ursula K., 112
LeShan, Eda J., 16
Lilly, John, 2
Logical reasoning, 86
Longfellow, Henry Wadsworth, 70
Long-range planning, 42
Loyal relationships, 87
Loyalty, 10

**M**

Manipulation, 26
Manipulators, 38
Materialism, 14
Mauriac, François, 118
Mediators, 65
Moment-by-moment living, 92-93
Montessori, Maria, x
Mood, FOURS and, 81
Moodiness, 10, 83
Morale, organizational, 55
Morality, ONES and, 101
Moralizers, 56
Moral relationships, 72-73
Moral thinking, 19
Motivation, 12
    feelings and, 36
    self and, 113
    in ONES, 19
    in TWOS, 25
    in THREES, 30-31
    in FOURS, 37
    in FIVES, 43
    in SIXES, 49
    in SEVENS, 55
    in EIGHTS, 61-62
    in NINES, 67
Motivators, 30, 31, 68

**N**

Naranjo, Claudio, 2
Natural laws, 77
Negotiation, 66
NINES, 65-69
    arrows of development for, 12
    chart of congruence for, 141
    key traits of, 131
    relational style of, 96-99
    wings of development for, 14

**O**

Objectivity, 14
Observers, 41-45
    color symbolism for, 103
ONES, 17-21
    arrows of development for, 10
    chart of congruence for, 133
    desire for accuracy by, 7

key traits of, 123
    relational style of, 72-75
    wings of development for, 13
Opportunism, 11
Opportunists, 32, 50
Optimism, 54
Organizational environment, 49
Organizational power, 60
Organizational skills, 19
Organizational structure, 42
Organizational vision, 43
Organizations
    commitment to, 89
    harmonious, 66, 67
    humanistic, 36
    leadership and, 61
    productivity in, 55
Overdependence, 12
Oversensitivity, 38

**P**

Passivists, 32
Passivity, 10, 68
Pavlova, Anna, 106
Peacefulness, 13
    maintaining, 67
Peacemakers, 50
People, rapport with, 24
People orientation, 23
Perfecters, 17-21
    color symbolism for, 101
Perfectionism, 11
Perfectionists, 56
Personal empowerment.
    See Empowerment
Personalists, 25, 36, 38
Personality.
    See also Enneagram types
    mixed, 8
    professional style and, 2
    of ONES, 17
    of TWOS, 23
    of THREES, 29
    of FOURS, 35
    of FIVES, 41
    of SIXES, 47
    of SEVENS, 53
    of EIGHTS, 59
    of NINES, 65
Personality core, 3, 15
Pessimism, 55
Pink, symbolism of, 101-102
Planning, long-range, 42
Playfulness, 14
Pleasure Seekers, 44
Positive attitude, 104
Positive thinking, 54
Possessiveness, 10
Potentialities, personal, 114-115

Present, consciousness of, 92
Principles
  of ONES, 19
  of TWOS, 24-25
  of THREES, 30-31
  of FOURS, 37
  of FIVES, 42-43
  of SIXES, 49
  of SEVENS, 55
  of EIGHTS, 61
  of NINES, 66-67
Problems
  avoidance of, 98
  denial of, 98
  minimization of, 68
Problem solving, 73.
  *See also* Team problem solving
  in TWOS , 76
  in THREES, 79
  in FOURS, 82
  in FIVES, 85
  in SIXES, 88
  in SEVENS, 91
  in EIGHTS, 94
  in NINES, 97
Procedural change, arbitrary, 74
Procrastination, 68, 74, 89, 91, 98
Producers, 29, 31
Productivity, 12
Professional decline
  of ONES, 20
  of TWOS, 26
  of THREES, 32
  of FOURS, 38
  of FIVES, 44
  of SIXES, 50
  of SEVENS, 56
  of EIGHTS, 62
  of NINES, 68
Professional development
  of ONES, 20
  of TWOS, 25
  of THREES, 31-32
  of FOURS, 37-38
  of FIVES, 43-44
  of SIXES, 49-50
  of SEVENS, 56
  of EIGHTS, 62
  of NINES, 67-68
Professional empowerment, 20.
  *See also* Empowerment
Professionals, Enneagram benefits to, 4-5
Professional style
  empowerment of, 37
  personal, 113-117
Purple, symbolism of, 102-103

## Q

Quality, concern with, 19

Quality Performer, 38
Quality performer work style, 17-18

## R

Rapport
  enhancing, 109-110
  in ONES, 74
  in TWOS, 76-77
  in THREES, 79
  in FOURS, 82
  in FIVES, 85
  in SIXES, 89
  in SEVENS, 92
  in EIGHTS, 95
  in NINES, 98
Receptionists, 65-66
Receptivity, 14
Reconcilers, 50, 66, 68
Red, symbolism of, 104
Rejection, fear of, 48, 81
Relaters, 31, 47-48
Relational styles, 71
Relationships
  Enneagram types in, 71-99
  sacrificing, 32
Relaxation, 13, 14
Responsiveness, 13, 14
Right hemisphere functions, 117
Rules, dislike of, 80

## S

Safety, need for, 103
Sand, George, 22
Schedule changes, 97
Self, uniqueness of, 3-4
Self-acceptance, 31, 83
Self-affirmation, 102
Self-assurance, 79
Self-awareness, 35, 37
Self-centeredness, 62
Self-determination, 61, 95
Self-discipline, 10, 11
Self-expression, 37
Self-image, low, 50
Self-integration, 116-117
Self-Seekers, 38
Self-sufficiency, 61
Sensitivity, 10, 12, 13
Serenity, experiencing, 74-75
SEVENS, 53-57
  arrows of development for, 11
  chart of congruence for, 139
  key traits of, 129
  relational style of, 90-93
  wings of development for, 14
"Shadow and light," 7, 9
Similarities, matching, 109-110
SIXES, 47-51

arrows of development for, 11
chart of congruence for, 138
key traits of, 128
relational style of, 87-90
wings of development for, 14
Social relationships, 90
Socrates, 2, 86
Solutions.
  See also Problem solving
  agreement on, 97
  workable, 94
Speaking
  professional, 54
  public, 91
Speculators, 62
Spiritual teachers, 2-3
Spontaneity, 55
Stability, 10
Stabilizer, 18, 38
Stoicism, 68
Sufism, 2
Supporters, 24, 25, 62
Systematizers, 42, 44, 56

T

Talents, developing, 15
Task orientation, 13, 14
Task-oriented relationships, 78
Team analysis, 110
Team effort, 88.
  See also Group mindedness
Team problem solving, 110-111
Teamsters, 31, 48, 50
Tender heartedness, 101-102
Thinkers, 41-42, 44, 56
Thinking style
  of ONES, 18-19
  of TWOS, 24
  of THREES, 30
  of FOURS, 36
  of FIVES, 42
  of SIXES, 48
  of SEVENS, 54
  of EIGHTS, 60
  of NINES, 66
THREES, 29-33
  arrows of development for, 10
  chart of congruence for, 135
  key traits of, 125
  relational style of, 78-79
  wings of development for, 13
Time

ONES' view of, 72-73
TWOS' view of, 75-76
THREES' view of, 78
FOURS' view of, 81
FIVES' view of, 84
SIXES' view of, 87
SEVENS' view of, 90
EIGHTS' view of, 93-94
NINES' view of, 97
Trustworthiness, 87
Truthfulness, 80
TWOS, 23-27
  arrows of development for, 10
  chart of congruence for, 134
  key traits of, 124
  relational style of, 75-77
  wings of development for, 13

U

Understanding, 11
  about relationships, 71
Universe, oneness with, 80
  See also Cosmic laws

V

Vision, organizational, 43
Visionaries, 62

W

White, symbolism of, 101
Whittier, John Greenleaf, 100
Wings of development, 8, 12-14
Wisdom, 86
Withdrawal, emotional, 87
Wordsworth, William, 64
Workaholism, 29, 32
Work style
  of ONES, 17-18
  of TWOS, 23, 26
  of THREES, 29
  of FOURS, 35-36
  of FIVES, 41-42
  of SIXES, 47-48, 50
  of SEVENS, 53-54
  of EIGHTS, 59-60
  of NINES, 65-66

Y

Yellow, symbolism of, 104